# Cāṇakya On Management

# Cāṇakya On Management

Ashok R. Garde

JAICO PUBLISHING HOUSE

Ahmedabad Bangalore Chennai
Delhi Hyderabad Kolkata Mumbai

Published by Jaico Publishing House
A-2 Jash Chambers, 7-A Sir Phirozshah Mehta Road
Fort, Mumbai - 400 001
jaicopub@jaicobooks.com
www.jaicobooks.com



CĀṆAKYA ON MANAGEMENT
ISBN 81-7992-408-4

First Jaico Impression: 2006
16th Jaico Impression: 2025



Printed by
Trinity Academy For Corporate Training Limited, Mumbai

# Foreword

It is nearly 30 months since I first read Prof. Ashok Garde's illuminating text titled "Canakya's Aphorisms on Management". Many will know Canakya as Chanakya, who was the mentor of the great Emperor Chandragupta Mourya of the 4th Century BC.

I then thought that the Business Schools should have it in their Library. Business School teachers are sure to find materials in it to support some presentation or the other on whatever subject is their prime concern.

I shall not comment on the contents except exhorting that whoever comes across this book should quickly read the "Introduction" because it succinctly describes its value to the reader. It may often result in that person wanting to own a copy for a serious reading.

I am glad that "Jaico Publishing House" is undertaking to popularize these Aphorisms amongst people all over India and abroad. Hopefully they shall aggressively promote its readership by encoura-ging the prestigious Business Schools such as the IIMs of India and the Ivy League B-Schools of USA and top Schools of Europe to order more than one copy for their library, because it is likely to be simultaneously used by several Professors and students.

In his introduction, the author has repeatedly referred to the book's utility to the CEO. I believe it will be useful for Managers at all levels and also the aspiring Managers. HR Managers should seriously consider procuring copies for study by their various functional heads. They can extract what appeals most to them for application in their area and having a "discussion" meeting with their peers or their reportees.

Mr. Ashok Garde was interviewed and selected by Dr. Vikram Sarabhai for the ATIRA job as a Scientist. But he soon learnt the art of management just as Dr.Vikram Sarabhai, a Scientist himself, became a highly successful Management Professional, who left his impact not only in the Private and Public Corporate organizations he served but also motivated people like Mr. Garde to become a great supporter of the Management movement in Ahmedabad. When AMA (Ahmedabad Management Association), founded by Dr. Vikram Sarabhai, proposed that ATIRA provide AMA a part of its spare land for housing the AMA Training and Development Center for the Working Managers and shared AMA's vision of making it the role model for various Local Management Associations (LMAs), who were members of the All India Management Association, Mr. Garde helped to work out a Win-Win situation for ATIRA, (whose Director he was), AMA and the people of Ahmedabad. Jaico may find the LMAs a useful means of popularizing the very valuable Management insights provided in this book.

Foreign Executives doing business with or in India do like to read about Indian culture and ethos. They will find this book interesting and will readily buy it but (and it is a big 'but') the question is that how will they know about the book and how can they easily get it. I do hope Jaico will work on seeing that it is available on the internet.

The author has written the sutras in the Sanskrit Devanagari Script and also in phonetic English script. If a reader pursues the book frequently he may find himself understanding several Sanskrit words. He or she may then read Panchatantra and Hitopadesa looking for morals for use In today's world of Management situation.

Today, as never before, more and more businessmen and Management gurus are talking about the importance of ethics, which, since time immemorial, the Indian thinkers and businessmen have highlighted as a must to be practiced in business and everyday conduct calling it "the arthashastra dharma" This "Dharma" has nothing to do with "religion" as is generally understood. Chanakya has a lot to say about the ethics and good governance

In India, the legendary Chanakya invokes respect bordering on awe. To scholars outside India, he is better known as Kautilya. He is the author of a full treatise on Governance. He practiced what he taught nearly 2400 years ago. He trained Chandragupta Mourya to be a fair, just and efficient Chief Executive Officer of a kingdom. His dynasty succeeded in making India attain great heights in all fields, with the Greek Commander in Chief of Alexander, the Great, getting his daughter married to Chandragupt Mourya.

Mr Garde has painstakingly brought out the manifold implications of each sutra. Experienced managers will note that many a sutras succinctly state a principle underlying their own experiences, but which they did not 'see' in that light before! The philosophical underpinning of managerial actions - any action - as propounded by Chanakya have been well brought out by the author. Consequently, those managers who work towards internalizing use-worthy sutras can become high achievers without being highly stressed by work.

With over 45 years of experience in top management and entrepreneurship, I feel that the ideas of Chanakya are worth following today, especially when adhering to the ethical path is the only 'mantra' to ensure long term survival and growth of an enterprise in a fiercely competitive globalised market. I hope that this book reaches a large number of managers in India and abroad and they benefit from it.

**P.V.R.N. IYER**<br>
President<br>
All India Management Association, New Delhi

Former Member<br>
Board of Governors of Indian Institute of Management, Ahmedabad

# Preface

Some management thinkers in India were looking for an Indian ethos in management, since neither the American nor the Japanese styles seemed to fit well into the Indian culture. I made a small attempt to look at *Pancatantra,* the world's first documented training programme for top management. Thereafter, I came across several popular Hindi versions of *Cāṇakya Sūtras.* Many appeared to be incorrectly interpreted, but quite a few were startlingly insightful and usable for guiding managerial actions.

By 1994, in the 4th year as the CEO of ATIRA, I started picking up a few sutras and using them as guide rules. Not all sutras are principles of management. Many are like 'laws of behaviour at work', indicating 'what will happen when' with a high probability. The flow of ideas is very different from the management thoughts of 1950s. In some ways, the total thought process is akin to the management thinking in the late 20th century, which includes *'what managers should **be**,* rather than only *'what managers should **do**'.* The idea that the manager should manage himself well on the emotional front has been seeping in gradually in the recent past.

The Indian ethos is visible all along in *Cāṇakya Sūtras*, and most concepts are meaningful in our current cultural context. This realisation led me to think of writing a commentary on *Cāṇakya Sūtras* from the management point of view. This desire was consistently reinforced by Shri KK Nair, Executive Director, AMA and Dr. Balabhaskaran, Dean, ICFAIAN Business School, Ahmedabad.

I am grateful to Shri Rajesh Mehta, President, AMA, and to Shri KK Nair for their decision to publish this work as an AMA publication. If the management personnel in India - the 'would be managers' and those practicing management professions at different levels - who read this book do just TWO things, the efforts of the author and of AMA will stand justified:

One: Discover a rather different way of looking at management.
Two: Check out which of these 216 aphorisms fit their experience.

If few of the readers do a Third - i.e. use selected sutras for guiding their actions - that would be great.

**Aśok Garde**

# Preface to Second Edition

**How to Get the Best of Canakya on Management**

A wide readership has shown appreciation for Canakya percepts on management: the first and second JAICO impressions have been sold out –nay, bought out – within about 90 days of release. This response has strengthened our belief that many *raja-neeti sutras* of Canakya are applicable to the process of management even today, in an industrially advanced society. The feedback received from several readers has indicated that it would be worthwhile to provide some guidelines on how to use the Canakya System in practice.

Firstly, the entire emphasis is on **wealth generation, its protection and growth** - with the help of several persons - **in an ethical manner**.

Secondly, these *sutras* are all about HOW a manager–especially, a CEO – can **groom himself/herself** for playing the role effectively, and successfully, without being mentally stressed.

Thirdly, the Canakya system is based on two kinds of **laws of management**: "X is a necessary condition for Y; but given X, Y may not follow inevitably" and "Given P, the consequence is Q; but Q may happen through other causes also." Examples of these types are: "1.1 Happiness is rooted in ethics' and '8.2 Giving of harsh punishments makes the manager hate-worthy by all'

These laws are different in nature from the various theories of management which have been formulated by management experts since about 1960. Each of these theory or technique, really useful for effectively managing large scale organisations functioning in market economy, has gained popularity for some years at a time till some other technique superceded it. Techniques would naturally depend on the way a business organisation has to function in a changing socio-economic and technological environment. Laws governing the human responses would not depend on such factors and would thus be valid universally over long periods.

**YOU can benefit most from Canakya System of Management by**

- Reading through quickly, without attempting to judge the applicability.
- Introspecting on own experiences in the context of *sutras* of YOUR interest.
- Committing to memory those few *sutras* which YOU find worthwhile.
- Internalizing the precepts from the memorized *sutras* by noting their applicability.
- Letting these *sutras* guide YOUR actions towards a more effective response to situations.

**Some *Sutra* Groups worth focusing YOUR attention for more effective management are:**

1. **Ethical Self Management:** 1.1 to 1.10
2. **Building Own Character:** 7.8, 8.8-9,12.5,12.9-10, 14.6-7, 16.10,17.5, 17.7-10, 19.4-5, 19.9-10, 20.1, 20. 4-10, 21.5-6
3. **Assessing Effectiveness of Management:** 4.1-8
4. **Philosophy for Work, Success/Failure:** 1.5-6, 10.3-6, 11.6-7 **(working without mental stress)**
5. **Aiming at Profits/Growth:** 7.11, 9.3-6
6. **Work : Project Planning/Policies:** 3.1-5, 3.8-12
7. **Dealing with Subordinates/Colleagues:** 8.1-2, 8.9-11, 13.7

You are welcome to use these sets of *sutras* as an initial step to derive advantage from this book.

## Writing and reading Sanskṛt in Roman Script

| देवनागरी | English | देवनागरी | English |
|---|---|---|---|
| अ | a | य् | y |
| आ | ā | र् | r |
| इ | i | ल् | l |
| ई | ī | व् | v |
| उ | u | श् | ś |
| ऊ | ū | ष् | ṣ |
| ए | e | स् | s |
| ऐ | ai | ह् | h |
| ओ | o | क्ष् | kṣ |
| औ | au | ज्ञ् | jn |
| अं | aṁ | | |
| अः | aḥ | | |

| | | | | | | | | | |
|---|---|---|---|---|---|---|---|---|---|
| क् | k | च् | c | त् | t | ट् | ṭ | प् | p |
| ख् | kh | छ् | ch | थ् | th | ठ् | ṭh | फ् | ph |
| ग् | g | ज् | j | द् | d | ड् | ḍ | ब् | b |
| घ् | gh | झ् | z | ध् | dh | ढ् | ḍh | भ् | bh |
| | | | | न् | n | ण | ṇ | म् | m |

Therefore, Cāṇakya = चाणक्य
*Sūtra* = सूत्र
*mūlaṁ* = मूलम्
*dharmaḥ* = धर्मः

# Contents

# Introduction

Management of people and of resources, whether for manufacturing products, or for providing services, or for administering a state, is a rather complicated task. Not surprisingly, therefore, we find that a plethora of *sets of generalisations* have been developed on "How to Manage Well to Achieve Excellent Results on a Sustainable Basis." Only a few of these have been total systems covering all the aspects of managing a business. Many have been applied to real life situations and used, but not necessarily well documented. The real test of a treatise on management is not just its completeness or just the beauty of its logic, but also the demonstration of its practical application in real life situations, with enduring success.

The well educated Indian, like his counterpart in the Western and now also in the Eastern world, is under the implicit impression that such systematic thinking on management started only in the 20th century. However, given the complexity of managing a kingdom or a country, it would not be surprising if treatises on management were written in the ancient past also. In fact, a search for such management literature in India and in the world yields fruitful results. Some of the well known works that deserve our attention are the following, listed in chronological order.[1]

| Author | Country | Treatise | Tutored | Approx. Period |
|---|---|---|---|---|
| Confucius | China | Analects | ? Prince of Lu | 430 BC |
| Aristotle | Greece | Politics | Alexander | 350 BC |
| Cāṇakya | India | Arthaśāstra | Candragupta | 330 BC |
| Viṣnuśarma/Bidāpi | India | Pancatantra | 3 princes | 200 BC |
| ? | India | Hitopadeśa | 3 princes | 200AD |
| Machiavelli | Italy | The Prince | ? | 1532 AD |

Whether the Zen and other oriental philosophies also had any parallel work on state craft per se' is doubtful. We will consider only the Indian treatises before focussing on the Cāṇakya-*sūtras*.

## Management: The Indian Ethos

The Pancatantra consists essentially of 69 case studies compiled by the Guru to teach *"management of people"* to three grown up sons of a king in a six-month residential training programme. Hitopadeśa is a similar treatise, that borrows heavily from Pancatantra, and has an identical narrative style. But unlike Arthaśāstra, these two deal only with one aspect of management - managing people. Cāṇakya's Arthaśāstra deals with all the different aspects of managing a kingdom, including management of men. Arthaśāstra is the earliest known and available treatise of this kind in the history of the world. The Cāṇakya *Sūtras* are an abstraction of the principles of management on which the treatise is based. In Arthaśāstra, Cāṇakya deals with all aspects of administering a state - from training and establishing a governing hierarchy, selecting people, and levying taxes, to laying down laws, to deciding punishments for breaking the law, etc. Incidentally, Cāṇakya - also known as Kautilya – refers to views of several earlier (over 600 years) Indian authorities on management. He then states his own view, giving reasons for differing from the earlier views. One presumes that he wrote the *Sūtras* with a view to make it easy for his students of management to remember the principles of management, in a manner that will prove useful in actual practice.

The Cāṇakya *Sūtras* have the unique distinction of being the principles which have been demonstrated to have been used successfully in practice to achieve good results on a sustainable basis. Cāṇakya taught these principles to a group of youths, including Candragupta, and used this well trained group to overthrow the unjust and oppressive dynasty of the Nanda kings of Pātaliputra, the capital of the country of Magadha. Candragupta established the Mourya dynasty, which ruled well for about 136 years, and produced a king like Samrāt Aśok (*samrāt* = great emporor). The successful installation of Candragupta, whose regime was fair and just, as opposed to the tyranny and partiality of the Nanda kings, is an eloquent testimony of the prowess of the management principles propounded by Cāṇakya. These principles, the Cāṇakya *Sūtras*, therefore, deserve a careful study in the present context, when we are on the lookout for an Indian ethos in management. The management principles used in the USA or in Japan are obviously derived from their own cultural background. There exists enough evidence already to show that these systems, even when meticulously and earnestly adopted in India, rarely take roots or produce the desired results on a sustainable basis. We do need to look for those principles that are likely to make sense in our own social and work culture. These would hopefully deliver better results for all concerned - the customers, the investors, the employees, the vendors, and the society.

Several of the current attempts at developing an Indian ethos in management turn to our philosophical or religious texts. Such efforts, though commendable, suffer from three disadvantages. Firstly, the philosophical religious texts were written primarily in the context of doing one's ordained duties as an individual. Secondly, these do not address the many different aspects of managing an enterprise. Thirdly, when we choose the scriptures of any one religion in India, the managers belonging to other religions find it really difficult to accept the concepts which are not to be found in the same form in their own religion. The basis for good management principles has to be secular and rational for universal acceptability. There exists no doubt that the principles propounded in Gīta are useful for individual managers to mould their own character, and to strengthen it for dealing effectively with problems faced by the managers. These are so rational that these can be accepted secularly without attributing God-ness to Kṛṣṇa. However, it is better to look at specifically management-oriented treatises like those cited above. From amongst these, the one complete system of looking at all aspects of management is the Cāṇakya-*Sūtras*.

### The *Sūtra* System

The *Sūtras* system of teaching or dealing with any body of knowledge is a unique system developed and used since about 7000 BC in India. A *Sūtra* is a short, pithy statement or an aphorism about a concept: it is easy to memorise, and to recall whenever required in practice. From Patanjali's *Yogasūtras** to Vātsyāyanā's *Kāmasūtras*, we see that the entire territory of the four *puruṣartha* has been covered by the *sūtras* system: these are *dharma, artha, kāma,* and *mokṣa* - duties/morals, resources/money, desires/sex, and salvation, respectively. The practicable knowledge and skills in each have been enunciated in the *sūtra* form also, besides in the textbook form. Each word in any *sūtra* is very carefully chosen.

It is important to note why only a specific word out of several possible has been chosen in any *sūtras*: omissions are as important as selections. The *sūtras* are stated one after another in a logical sequence, and the number of *sūtras* on a specific topic/idea do not exceed 15 or so. This number of *Sūtras* per topic is variable - it ranges from 2 to 20, but is generally between 6 and 12. The sequencing of topics by itself is an interesting commentary on the scheme of teaching developed by the teacher, or adopted by the author. Since authorship without being a teacher was rare in India in those times, we will consider *sūtras* as propounded by a person playing the role of a teacher.

The teacher/guru would narrate a set of *sūtras* to the students *(śiṣya)*, who would repeat them aloud several times till these get fully memorised. These would be recited later to confirm the ability to recall at will, and to ensure accuracy, or fidelity, in reproduction. The guru would comment upon the meaning and implications of each *sūtra* in practice, and would demonstrate each behavioural principle also through his own behaviour. The guru thus succeeded in making the disciples internalise the principles so well, that they would never forget to apply them in practice, and would behave accordingly. In other words, any *sūtra* needs to be commented upon, and interpreted for correct understanding and use. The commentary in the present exercise will focus on the ideas on management as understood in the present industrial context, while showing linkages with Indian cultural perceptions in general.

## Interpreting *Sūtras*

Seven specific considerations have to be taken note of in the present interpretation of Cāṇakya's principles of management.

1. About 200-220 *sūtrās* from the set of over 450 *sūtras* is meant to teach the principles of management to the rulers and the administrators of kingdoms: the rest are meant for the common man. The *sūtrās* on management are therefore more directly applicable to the functioning of the IAS/IPS/IFS categories of civil services. These were not meant to be applicable to running of business enterprises. However, as is also being considered in the present times, many principles of management are commonly applicable to both. Consequently, in interpreting words such as kingdom, servants etc., we will use words such as the enterprise, employees, etc. Interpreting relations with neighbouring countries, or with enemies, in business terms gives rise to some difficulties, and these need to be accepted.

2. The first 160-180 *sūtras* in the authoritative text of Cāṇakyasūtrani happen to be directly on *rāja-nīti* or *rājya-tantra* i.e. on management. Thereafter, one finds a mixture of a sort, where *sūtras* on management appear intermittently between *sūtras* on general good behaviour for the 'gentlemen' in a civilised society. These have been picked up and formed into further chapters in the present compilation. It needs also to be acknowledged that the chapterisation seen in this book is the author's superimposition on the authoritative text. The original sequence of appearance of *sūtras* has been followed almost invariably. Because of this, in some chapters, a *sūtra* or two may be found to be non-fits, if not clearly mis-fits. Such oddities need to be accepted and tolerated as a consequence of chapterisation not originally intended by Cāṇakya.

3. Given the rich language that Saṅskṛt is, each word has very many different meanings. We will select the meaning(s) most appropriate in the context, but will not stretch any meaning to suit our current perception, or to bring about conformity with them. After all, if we find a principle or a percept to be not relevant in present times, we are at liberty to not follow it - to disregard it!

4. Typically, the *sūtras* do not show forms of the verb "to be" in the sentences: this helps to reduce the number of words, is consistent with the common usage of the Saṅskṛt language, and also helps to connect to the next *sūtras* while remembering the *sūtras* by rote. In situations where the meaning is to be explicit, the forms of this verb are included in the text explicitly.

5. Some *sūtras* are clearly seen to be non-relevant to the topic under consideration. These are likely to be misplaced in the text, or unauthorised later insertions, or possibly a result of faulty succession through the memory route. These will be cited - not omitted - but will not be commented upon in detail. When found to be placed at a wrong position, a *sūtra* will be transferred to a place more consistent with the concept being elaborated upon.

6. Most *sūtras* are written in such a manner that the person (or self) involved could either be a man or a woman. We will always use the masculine form 'he' because there was no likelihood of women being trained to rule at the time of Cāṇakya. However, the reader would do well to interpret the masculine as equally applicable to the feminine. No gender bias is either intended or implied in this method of writing, adopted mainly for convenience. We know that

women can become as good managers as men can.

7. As a matter of 'policy', the author had decided not to read 'Arthaśāstra'[2] of Kautilya before attempting to interpret his *sūtras* on management. The main reason was to preserve the ability to think independently of the cultural context of the time period in which these *sūtras* were written. Therefore, only the relevant 'dictionary' meanings were used in understanding the words of these *sūtras*. However, just as a language dictionary of the present times does not give the technical meanings of some words used in the different branches of sciences, the specific technical meanings were not to be found in the dictionary. Consequently, whenever some important words were defined differently in '*rajya-tantra* (as propounded in Arthaśāstra) the interpretation given by this author became rather different from the meanings which Cāṇakya wished to convey. The four important words where such a difference occurred are: *dharma, vinaya, prakṛti* and *mantra*. Fortunately, and possibly by chance if not by design of the original author, these 'common word' based interpretations by the present author turn out to be meaningful in the ancient as well as in current concepts of management of an enterprise or a nation. Therefore, both these versions have been retained in the text, ensuring that the reader is clearly aware of the meanings of these words as used in Arthaśāstra.

Incidentally, the *sūtras* will be written in a form where words are separately shown for ease of understanding and spelling. This will also make it easier to those who are less familiar with Saṅskṛt. Fortunately, the words used by Cāṇakya are simple: many of them are being commonly used in most Indian languages even today.

A few words about the currently available 'modern' commentaries on Cāṇakya-*Sūtras* are in order before we proceed. The reference here is to the paperbacks available in Hindi as popular editions. Apparently, Saṅskṛt Pandits, who have never held any managerial or administrative position, have written these commentaries. No manager or management teacher has apparently turned to Cāṇakya's principles on management. Moreover, the *Saṅskṛt* Pandits have tended to interpret this work also in spiritual context, for reasons best known to them! These translations-cum-commentaries thus suffer not only from mis-reading of the text, but also from addition of thoughts and ideas alien to the subject under consideration.

The given name of the author of the Cāṇakya-*Sūtras* is *Viṣṇugupta*: but he was mostly known as Cāṇakya, being the son of *Caṇaka*. Later, he also came to be known as Kautilya, meaning "the one who advocated *kutilnīti*" (crooked/cunning ways).Western schools have compared him with Machiavelli, the 16th century Italian statesman-advisor to kings. Machiavelli is so well known for advocating unscrupulous methods to retain/gain power, that the English language has acquired the phrase ' Machiavellian methods`! It would prove interesting to the readers of Cāṇakya-*Sūtras* to find out which one or more of the 455 *Sūtras* indicate any crooked or unethical advice by *Viṣṇugupta*: i.e. Cāṇakya, the first management guru of the world. There is none whatever! In his treatise on Arthaśāstra, he does advise the king several ways of protecting himself, and several ways of acting against the enemy which are definitely manipulative and often unethical. However, within his own kingdom, he is a strong advocate of ensuring ethical behaviour of all levels through appropriate legal enforcements. Throughout his treatise, he prefers to refer to himself (as the author) as Kautilya. Kautilya, the son of *Caṇaka*, is the first, and perhaps the only, management guru who propounded principles, taught them, trained persons and made them managers who managed well for long years. He was also the only one who dissociated himself from enjoying the fruits of his efforts, by retiring as soon as *Candragupta* was established as a king.

# Invocation

सा श्रीः वः अव्यात् ।

*sa śrīh waḥ avyāt*

May that wealth protect you (all)

The beginning of any good work is with an invocation. The invocation above is to wealth, for protection: "May that wealth protect you all."

Besides meaning wealth, or plenty/prosperity, *śrī* also stands for dignity, any virtue or excellence, intellect/understanding, and fame/glory amongst others. And the verb form *avyāt* also means to do good to, to promote/animate, to give pleasure to, etc., besides to protect. We may, therefore, also consider the following possible other meanings of this invocation.

- May that excellence do well to you all.
- May that understanding animate you all.
- May that glory give pleasure to you all.

Too many permutations are possible! And all of them are seen to make good sense. It is commonly believed (and also done) that invocations are to be addressed to God or to an eternal spirit in the religious/spiritual sense. This invocation is totally different: these are good wishes of a teacher for his pupils.

'That wealth/excellence/understanding/glory that you generate may protect/do good to/enthuse/give pleasure to you all': are the best wishes-cum-messages of the guru to his *śiṣya* (disciples).

It is significant to note that the Guru does not see himself as a beneficiary of the resultant prosperity. Cāṇakya could as well have used the pronoun *nah* instead of *wah,* where *nah* stands for 'we all'. This basic fact is important: the teacher is not teaching anything to students for his own benefit, even if it were to come along with the benefits to students themselves. He dissassociates himself from the prosperity that will result through his teachings, because benefiting from that prosperity is neither his goal nor his desire.

Mark also the focus on wealth generation, working for excellence, for achieving wisdom and glory. Protecting oneself is not possible in a civilised society unless one has this possession named *śrī.* Note also the fact that this teacher of management invokes wealth itself before starting to say anything about management per se'. Wealth generation is valued, neither looked down upon nor deprecated at all.

CHAPTER

# 1 ॥ मूलानि ॥ Foundations

1 सुखस्य मूलं धर्मः ।

*sukhasya moolam dharmah (asti)*

Basis of happiness (is) ethics.

(The implicit verb *'asti'* is shown in brackets, and the corresponding meaning "is" in the translation is also shown in brackets. This is just to illustrate the style of writing *sūtras*. Next *sūtra* onwards, this will not be done.)

The word mūlam means a root, a beginning/commencement, or basis/foundation/origin. Take any of these senses, the message is clear. *'dharma'* is the basis of happiness: i.e. *sukhaṁ*. *Sukhaṁ* also means prosperity, welfare, good health, alleviation of sorrow, comfort, etc. The word *'dharma'* is used here not in the sense of religion, but in the sense of prescribed duty, or code of conduct. The meaning of the word *dharma* has been elaborated upon by Kautilya in Arthaśāstra: it consists of three aspects of behaviour of all human beings. The first refers to the duties to be performed by persons belonging to different *varṇas" Brahmaṇa, Kṣatriya, Vaiśya, Śudra*. Learning, teaching, priesthood etc. for *Brahmaṇas*; learning, protecting etc. for *Kṣatriyas*; commerce, agriculture, animal rearing for *Vaiśyas;* and all services, artisonships, and entertainment etc. for the *Śudras* (These 'occupations' were not rigidly tied with birth in specific *varṇa* at that time). The second aspect refers to the four stages of life of every individual from any *varṇa;* the *aśrama* system. *Brahmacarya, gruhastha, vānaprastha,* and *sanyāsa,* are the four periods of 20-25 years of every one's life devoted to studying/training; becoming a family man contributing to the society; dissassociating oneself from total involvement, and lastly, giving up everything to concentrate on spirituality respectively. The third aspect is a code of conduct for all individuals in any civilised society. Cāṇakya lists six virtues of behaviour which all must follow all the time. These are *ahimsa, satya, śauca, anasūya, anṛsansya* and *kṣama*: i.e. non-violence, truth, cleanliness (of body and mind), non-jealousy, non-cruelty and forgivance. The choice of *varṇa* is left to the individual in all democracies of the present day, while the ideas of *aśrama* system manifest themselves in the lives of most people in the world if their livelihood is secured. In the context of happiness of all in a society, it is the third aspect – the three positive and the three non-negative aspects of the behaviour of an individual in a society listed by Cāṇakya —which defines *dharma*. The nearest word that describes and encompasses all these meanings succinctly is ethics. In the context of management, the word *dharma* will be translated simply by the word ethics in the entire course of this commentary.

It is remarkable that the very first *sūtra* of a management treatise starts with 'happiness' - not with money, nor fame, nor success. It refers to happiness, as distinct from pleasure. Indeed, what each individual human being, living in the society to which he/she belongs, really wants is to be happy. The sole purpose of all endeavours of management is to generate happiness for all: not just for the rulers/managers, but also for the subjects/employees. It is stressed that ethical behaviour alone can be the foundation for such a result to take place: i.e. an allround happiness can be experienced by all in the society.

Ethical behaviour is universal, while moral behaviour is often defined by the particular culture of the society. In other words, morals are culture specific, while ethics is the same for all human beings. Ethical behaviour can be defined by two simple criteria, which would be acceptable the world over. (Reference: Human Society in Ethics, by Bertrand Russell). We consider here only those actions of individuals that have some effect on one or more other individual human beings. All other actions are ethically neutral.

1. Consider a person A, who becomes happy by doing action X that affects another person B. If A becomes happy also by the same action X done to A by B, then the action X is an ethical action.

2. Consider an action Y, taken by A to make himself happy, that affects the entire society in which he lives. If all in that society were to take the same action Y, will all individuals in the society feel happy? If yes, then the action Y is ethical. If all in the society were to take the same action Y, will the society continue to function or survive in the long run? If yes, the action Y is ethical.

As will be noted, the second criterion above is the corollary of the first. A large part of the ethical behaviour is also considered as moral behaviour; while some moral behaviour is ethically neutral. Most prescribed codes of conduct are laid down by common consent in a community/society/nation and also by religious tenets. These moral codes are almost always drilled into the minds of individuals in their early childhood by their parents and by teachers at schools. These consist of ethical elements as well as purely moral elements. Only a small fraction of these ethical moral tenets are made legal by the society, whereby a penalty is prescribed and is enforceable in case of any breach of the code. As will be seen from the *sūtras* that follow, the appropriate meaning of *dharma* is the idea of ethics as defined by the twin criteria given above.

Cāṇakya, whose father had suffered injustice from the Nanda kings, knew the value of ethical behaviour by the rulers for the happiness of their subjects, from his first hand experience. And of course, the traditions of the Raghu dynasty in ancient India, which produced great kings like Bharata and Rāma, as well as the teachings of the Vidur Nīti[4] from Mahābhārata were known since about 3000 years before Cāṇakya. In China, Confucius had propagated the ideas of an ethically run state in the 6th Century BC. Thiruvelluvar, in Tamilnadu of today, who wrote Thirukkural[5] just about 300 years after Cāṇakya, can be considered to be the first saint-poet who brought such ideas to reach the common man by putting them in simple, but elegant verse form. The saint-poets of the period 800 AD to 1700 AD in several languages of India have conveyed this type of thinking about ethics and happiness in simple language. This rich heritage of the regional languages of India has led to a very interesting consequence. A large majority of Indians today - from all economic levels of the society and from different religions, including those who are illiterate - have a built-in thinking about what is fair and just, therefore, ethical. The concept that happiness comes out of behaving ethically is a common perception all over the world, and especially so in India because of the influence of the saint-poets on the common man.

## 2 धर्मस्य मूलम् अर्थः ।

*dharmasya mūlaṁ arthaḥ*

Basis of ethics is resources.

Neither following the ethical path nor performing one's duties to others is a behavioural pattern which is possible until the individual concerned has the money or the means - resources - to fulfil the minimum needs of food, clothing and shelter. Therefore, immediately after stating the need for ethics, the rulers/managers are told the profound truth that they should not expect subjects/ employees to adopt ethical behaviour unless they are well fed, clothed, and housed. One must first have (be provided with) the minimum resources for satisfying the three basic needs.

Indian culture has always emphasised what is stated in the first two *sūtras* taken together - namely, that money does not lead directly to happiness. Happiness for self and others results through ethical behaviour: money or resources make ethical behaviour possible. "*dhanāt dharmah tataḥ sukhaṁ*" is a refrain all over India since time immemorial.

We are all familiar with the story 'Les Miserable' by Victor Hugo: can we really accuse the hungry poor boy who stole the apple, of unethical behaviour and punish him for theft? Managers need to note that the employees at the lowest level need to be well taken care of before they can be expected to follow rules. It is, of course, clear, that "satisfaction of minimum needs" is necessary, but not a sufficient condition for any person to follow the ethical path.

This also means that one must strive to generate wealth - resources, money - and share it with all equitably to create happiness for oneself and others. Such generation of wealth must also be through ethical means, which alone would lead to overall happiness. Every one who wishes to gain something, starts with the words *śubha* and *lābha*: *śubha* means good/auspicious, and *lābha* means gain/profit. It is worth noting that even the crooked amongst the Indian traders know that *śubha* comes first, and *lābha* comes afterwards!

3 अर्थस्य मूलम् राज्यम् ।

*arthasya mūlaṁ rājyaṁ*

Basis of resources is kingdom (enterprise).

Resources can be controlled, surplus generated and used for different purposes through the possession of a kingdom. One governs a territory, levies taxes in return for protection from enemies/thieves, and also for providing common amenities, thereby justifying the need for a kingdom to exist.

A parallel that we can see is creating wealth through business activities - especially industrial activities. Trade does not generate wealth. Farmers, who produce different crops, and cattlemen/shepherds/poultry farmers are the persons who generated wealth in the past and continue to do so even today. The development of science, technology and engineering, taken together with the market economy which fosters competition amongst creators of wealth, has resulted in a tremendous development in two distinctly different modes of wealth generation which were unknown at the time of Cāṇakya. These modes are the industry and the services sectors. The large nation states of today are similar in structure to the kingdoms, but are governed by the elected representatives of the people. We now have very large-scale enterprises in the agriculture, industry and service sectors.

It would, therefore, be appropriate to use the word enterprise as a substitute for the word kingdom here. It would indeed be interesting to study whether the principles of management specifically put down for training of rulers about 2300 years ago are usable in the rather different context, and in the vastly large scale of operations that exist today.
We have already seen that this entire concept of looking at management – the essential philosophy and the explicit thought process - is very different from the current study of management. The very first 3 *Sūtras* are philosophical generalisations not considered even relevant in modern teaching of managements. It is only since 1980s that the management have started emphasising ethical behaviour. And the connection to the society through social responsibility started becoming important even later. The management courses offered by many schools in the USA have Business Ethics as a course of study. Only one management school in India has Business Ethics and Corporate Governance as a compulsory course for their 2-year programme. However, we must also note that good industrial management houses had implemented both these aspects as early as in the beginning of the 20th century, including in India.

## 4 राज्यमूलम् इंद्रियजयः ।

*rājyamūlam indriyajayaḥ*

Enterprise is rooted in conquering (body) organs.

While the concept of enterprise being the basis of resources follows directly after the idea of resources as the basic requirement for following ethics, here we see an entirely unexpected turn in the thought process. From the impersonal, almost philosophical statements of universal truths on societal good, we suddenly enter an individual's personal domain. Our current schools of management talk of management of every 'thing', but not really of managing the 'self' for becoming a manager. In the holistic thinking of Cāṇakya, the management cannot possibly be separated from the manager: only when the manager knows how to govern himself, can he hope to manage others according to the laid down/ prescribed principles of management. This holistic thinking is in keeping with the traditions of the past at his time, and with the thinking in the orient in general. The Indian culture, even today, emphasises 'control' on self, without the control having to be suppressive. So, this fourth *sūtra* 'naturally' follows the third, while in the modern way of thinking on management, we find this sequence rather unexpected!

Victory over the organs of the body', which is the literary meaning of the word *indriyajayah*, is a well-known concept in our culture. An appropriate control over the five organs of sense (eyes, ears, tongue, nose, and skin), and on the five organs of action (hands, feet, mouth, genitals, and anus) is obviously expected from all mature, adult persons irrespective of their status and role in any society. Each grown up individual does control the impulses to indulge in unrestricted gratification of pleasure derived from these organs, especially in the context of not hurting others in the process. The manager, who gets to control much greater resources than most in the society, is in a position of power. As an individual, he/she can hurt the interest of others with much greater force, and also with a rather large extent of immunity from adverse consequences. All the more reason why the manager should be told that he/she must control himself/herself with much greater effort if the enterprise is to be managed well in a sustainable manner. Conquering the body organs is manifested through control over the '6 enemies' of the mind - *kāma, krodha, lobha, mada, moha, matsara* i.e. desires, anger, greed, arrogance, infatuation and envy. Cāṇakya mentions *māna* (pride/ego) and *harṣa* (pleasure) in place of *moha* and *matsara* as the last two of these.

Only if the manager has conquered the organs of his body would he be able to put the goals of the organisation first, especially when in conflict with self-interest. Only a mature manager understands that his self-interest is best served, in the long run, through fulfilling organisational goals all the time, without exception.

## 5 इन्द्रियजयस्य मूलम् विनयः ।

*indriyajayasya mūlam vinayah*

Conquering organs is rooted in moral training/humility.

The temptation to yield to gratification of pleasures derivable from the bodily organs is strong: especially with disregard to its short-term consequences to others, and without realising the long-term consequences to self. The temptation is all the greater if one is in position of power. That 'power corrupts' is a universal observation amongst all cultures in the world, from the primitive to the most civilised. The philosopher-poet-king Bhartruhari[6] has propounded an excellent hypothesis on why 'good advice' does not get used, though really useful to those in need. He says" The learned are smitten with jealousy, those in power positions are spoiled by arrogance, and the rest are too badly hit by ignorance!" Cāṇakya teaches his management trainees to cultivate humility, while seeking positions of power to govern or to manage. Not letting power to generate arrogance, however well concealed from others, takes quite some moral strength. The common meaning of the word *vinaya* is humility; but this term is used by Cāṇakya as a technical term with specific meaning of 'training in morality' which is also 'self-discipline to be ethical'. In fact, the very first chapter of Arthasastra is named '*vinaya-adhikarikam* i.e. the book of moral training'. The ruler/manager is expected to study four knowledge disciplines philosophy, three vedas and history, economics/finance and law/justice/enforcement system. The philosophical part consists of the two schools of *sānkhya* and *yoga*, besides *lokāyata*, the school which is atheist, or as least agnostic. Without such a philosophical basis, internalising of ethical and moral principles would really not be easy to sustain.

It is in such a context that *indriyajaya* – conquest of organs is rooted in self-discipline resulting from training in ethics and morals. Ethical capabilities are needed to distinguish between the right action and the wrong action, when facing job of defining without ambiguity and without any subjectiveness (in the sense of dependence on the person) what is 'right' or 'ethical' is not easy. Given a specific societal culture, what is 'morally right' is usually known: this may be consistent with ethics or may even be downright non-ethical/un-ethical. It takes a great strength of character to follow the right ethically and/or morally, when it hurts some pleasures of organs in the short term, but is in the interest of happiness in the long term. It takes even a greater strength of character to decide the 'right' action when the ethical and moral aspects conflict with each other. An ethically and morally strong character is a must for a ruler/manager for two purposes: he must always be able to put the 'good of the organisation' first, not his own interests. And he must be able to generate trust in himself and loyalty to the organisation in the people whom he leads.

The manager thus needs to be trained to discipline himself first. Cāṇakya considers this kind of training in self-discipline, cultivating humility, and following the ethical/moral path as a science by itself.

Unless one has basic, built-in humility, one will neither see nor observe occurrences around one in their true perspective: an arrogant mind will either filter uncomfortable observations or distort them to suit ones intentions and views. Nor will one listen to what others - individuals or groups - have to say, though hearing them out ostensibly: pre-conceived notions would normally distort what such an arrogant person understands from others. The arrogant manager, full of self-importance, and convinced of his own point of view, will not be capable of listening, seeing, feeling, (smelling and tasting, too) in a detached and non-involved manner. Obviously, neither his interpretation of the nature of the situation, nor his diagnosis can be consistently appropriate and effective. Consequently, the actions taken by him for achieving the desired results cannot reliably lead to the expected results.

Cultivation of a basic humility in the doer of actions even when his actions are seen to be giving the expected results, is yet another cultural tenet of the Indian sub-continent. In fact, humility is a virtue emphasised in every single oriental teaching.

Success is the word we use when we get the desired results from any effort. The *Sāṅkhya* philosophy (about 5000 BC) quoted in Gīta[7] (about 3000 BC), states that any action whatsoever can take place only when five elements are present. These are: basis for action (*adhiṣṭhānaṁ*), the doer of action (*kartā*), the means for action (*karaṇaṁ*), the efforts by the doer (*ceṣṭā*), and chance (*daivaṁ*). The elements doer, means, efforts are clear: these are the only three that we normally think of. Implicitly assumed is the first element of basis. If one were to attempt to convert a stone into gold, the efforts of this doer would have no basis, whatever the means adopted! The fifth element chance is neither expected by us, nor liked, because it takes away the credit from the doer. The literal translation of the word *daiva* would perhaps be fate, but there is no concept of any pre-determined fate involved in this discussion of actions by a doer. Nor is any God-given outcome meant here, because no ways are prescribed to propitiate any god.

The right meaning of *daiva* here is chance: chance is in fact a confluence of several factors – quite beyond the control of the doer – that influence the results of any action. Since the doer cannot control the results, the doer cannot be certain that the desired result will take place. So, no doer should consider that he by himself has achieved the results, even if he were to be successful - i.e. were to get the desired results - most of the time. This is the basic humility that the doer has to learn, and has to be continuously aware of. Otherwise, the doer tends to take the credit for himself for all successes, and to blame other person(s) or event(s) for every failure. The doer thereby starts to believe that the results are his doings, and thus he perpetuates the myth of his capabilities, leading to arrogance.

The *yoga* philosophy, contemporary of *sānkhya*, propounds that a doer should detach himself from the results of actions' in the sense that he should perform his duties of all types with enthusiasm and involvement, but without being concerned about whether the efforts will give the desired or undesired results. All experiences such as happiness/sorrow, gains/losses, victory/defeat, hot/cold etc. should be taken with equanimity. That is, react to events naturally as they happen, but do not dwell upon them too long. Do not remain 'attached' to such events of good (leading to happiness) or of bad (leading to unhappiness) type in terms of the past or of the future. It is emphasised that either of the two paths of *sankhya* or *yoga* lead to the same state of control over self.

How does one go about self-disciplining oneself in ethical/moral ways to be able to conquer the organs?

## 6 विनयस्य मूलम् वृद्धोपसेवा ।

*vinayasya mūlaṁ vruddhopasevā*

Moral training is based in serving the elders.

The words *vruddha* and *upasevā* have specific meanings in the context of the training-cum-teaching system followed since time immemorial in India. The process of education consisted of the teacher giving information and knowledge on the subject matter simultaneously with cultivating appropriate attitudes and behavioural patterns. This ensured that the acquired knowledge would be used in the right manner and fruitfully in the society. Thus, teaching of knowledge and training in skills took place simultaneously in a residential school controlled by the teacher - the guru. The students -disciples/*śiśya* - not only studied there, but also served by way of performing duties needed to maintain the school (*āśrama*), themselves, and the teacher's family.

Cāṇakya emphatically maintains that true humility, and control of sense organs through right moral behaviour can be cultivated only by learning from persons more learned than oneself in the area of ones interest; and that too, by being with the learned person with an attitude of serving under him. This respectful attitude towards the teacher, whose wisdom one wishes to acquire by being with him, is quite different from the process of hiring a knowledgeable individual to impart information.

The word *vruddha* stands for greater in age as well as greater in knowledge, skill, wisdom, etc. The word *upa-seva* stands for serving by being near. King Bhartruhari has another observation on those who acquire knowledge." When I learnt a few things, I became puffed up, like an elephant in heat, as if I am a know-all. But when I came in contact with the wise, I suddenly realised that I am a fool, and my arrogance disappeared like fever treated by medicine." Indeed, there is nothing like juxtaposition with the learned and the wise to generate the requisite humility.

Moral strength comes not just from a cognitive acknowledgement of the difference between the right and the wrong: it requires courage of conviction and of action to choose the right when the time comes. Observing those respected in the society in situations where they choose between the right and the wrong helps in a big way. Whether it is George Washington learning to tell the truth about the axe; Martin Luther King taking up the cause of his brethren; Mahatma Phule fighting to get the untouchables admitted to Hindu temples; or Mahatma Gandhi breaking the salt-tax law; it is the examples set by these men with great moral strength that inspired others to follow the path of righteousness in the interest of the society. Similarly, it takes a wise guru to instil morality in his disciples through his setting of right examples. In fact, the teacher has to be a role model for the students when it comes to teaching ethics: no other way seems to have been discovered by mankind for this!

A major task of the guru was to inculcate the spirit of being fair and just - behaving ethically correctly - amongst the students under his care. Naturally, several other moral injunctions were also expected to be ingrained. To illustrate: one tenet was to treat the *gurupatni* - teacher's wife - like ones own mother, and consider her as well, to be a goddess like one's own mother was expected to be revered. Many of these would be ethically neutral. We need to note that such culture specific moral tenets would change over time even in a given society, besides being different between different societies.

A well-known *śubhāṣita* (good saying, in verse form) is worth quoting at this stage to demonstrate how these ideas on humility, wealth, and happiness get connected in the Indian culture.

*vidyā dadāti vinayaṁ, vinayād yāti pātratā; pātratwāt dhanaṁ apnoti, dhanāt dharmaḥ tataḥ sukhaṁ*

The sequence is as follows: knowledge imparts humility/morality, thence comes capability, which begets wealth, wealth permits ethical behaviour, leading to happiness. The consistency with which this sequence of concepts is found to occur in the Indian thought is indeed surprising, and gratifying.

## 7 वृद्धोपसेवया विज्ञानम् ।

*vruddhopasevayā vijnānaṁ*

Worldly knowledge through serving with the learned.

As Bertrand Russell, amongst others, has pointed out, the word *jnyāna* was used by the ancients - whether from Egypt, Greece, Rome, or Bharat (India) - to denote that body of knowledge which explained the purpose of life in the universe. It was not to be used for understanding nature, and to predict the outcomes of various natural phenomena. In other words, *jnyāna* was used for philosophical knowledge, rather than for scientific knowledge. The word *vijnyāna*, on the other hand, stands not only for understanding, prediction, and control of the physical, chemical, biological phenomena, but also for similar understanding of human behaviour. Cāṇakya uses the word *vijnyāna* presumably to denote this worldly knowledge of both kinds.

The right way to acquire this worldly knowledge is prescribed as follows. Be with the learned, serve them as they demonstrate their precepts through their own behaviour, learn cognitively first, and then internalise the teachings of the teacher. The knowledge involved here consisted naturally of administration of a country: collection of revenue and taxes, law and order, punishment to legal offenders, and setting up a system to permit the entire state apparatus to function smoothly. (This body of knowledge would not deal with the sciences of mathematics, chemistry, civil and mechanical engineering, etc. which were known at that time in India. Possibly, these would need to be considered in the context of giving state patronage to the practitioners of these sciences and crafts.) This interpretation of the word *vijnyāna* in this *sūtra* is derived from Cāṇakya's exposition in his treatise *"artha-śāstra"*, where he deals with these and many other aspects of administering a country. A careful reader will find that the order in which these *sūtras* begin is the same as that used in the treatise.

In the first book named *'vinaya-adhikarikaṁ* on training, Kautilya (as Cāṇakya preferred to address himself in Arthaśāstra) states that the manager should learn four *vidya*: *anvikṣiki, veda, vārtta* and *danda-nūti*. That is: philosophy consisting of *sānkhya, yoga* and *lokāyata* (atheism); three vedas which specify duties of *varṇa* and *aśrama* plus *itihasa-veda* (history); economics as we define today; and law and legal enforcement. Cāṇakya has not used the word *vidyā* in this or other *sūtras*. He has preferred to use the word vijnyana, which perhaps emphasises the worldly wisdom of dealing with people when putting the *vidyās* to use.

In our present application of these *sūtras*, we will therefore interpret the word *vijnāna* as "the knowledge of how to manage an enterprise through managing well trained persons towards generation of wealth."

This idea of fostering self growth towards excellence in management through being under the guidance of a successful senior manager is not uncommon at all. It happens to be a well-recognised method for real life learning even today. In their book on "Search for Excellence"[8], Thomas Peters and Robert Walterman have pointed out that 'having someone as your mentor in the organisation you work' has been found to be one of the major ingredients of excellence in management. The mentor not only demonstrates principles from his own practice, but also provides timely and appropriate feedback on how to improve performance. The mentor advises on areas/topics need to be studied/ mastered, and provides opportunities for undertaking successively more difficult/ responsible tasks with corresponding accountability.

8 विज्ञानेन आत्मानम् संपादयेत् ।

*vijnānena ātmānaṁ saṁpādayet*

Equip yourself fully with worldly knowledge.

This is the first time that a directive is being given to the students by their guru. The first seven *sūtras* stated general principles for understanding by the students. The disciples are emphatically told that it is in their own interest to take efforts towards acquiring the requisite knowledge from the mentor. After all, the general principle stated in the earlier *sūtra* - gaining knowledge through serving the learned - is not expected to take place on its own. Nor it is the responsibility of the teacher to instil his knowledge in the students. The onus of learning is entirely on the students. This aspect of the student being desirous of learning, and his approaching the right kind of person as a mentor to help him grow professionally, is important to understand and remember all the time. Obviously, the truth that it is not the need of the teacher to teach (for earning his own living, for example) but that of the student to learn, which must be understood unambiguously. Humility, consequently, is a built-in part of the management education.

The verb *saṁ-pad* stands not only for acquiring of the worldly knowledge, but also for enriching oneself with it. Acquisition of worldly knowledge is in itself an enrichment of the self towards a better performance at the tasks to be undertaken. Cognitive acquisition of the worldly knowledge followed by internalisation leading to appropriate behaviour in practice is meant to be conveyed by this *sūtra*. The stress is on the student to be proactive in learning.

## 9 संपादितात्मा जितात्मा भवति ।

*sampāditātmā jitātma bhavati*

One who has acquired knowledge becomes one who has conquered himself.

The fourth *sūtra,* which states that an enterprise can be built only on the basis of control of organs, was the first turn towards the manager as a person for the focus of improvement. This nineth *sūtra* completes the process by making a profound generalisation. Only those who have equipped themselves well with the knowledge of the world will be in full control of their own self. Only such persons will be able to conquer the 'six enemies' (1.4) which distort the intellect and reason when not well controlled.

Cāṇakya does not feel the need to enjoin the student, to urge the student who has acquired the right type of worldly knowledge through humbly serving the teacher, to control himself totally. He knew that the *guru-śiśya* (teacher-student) learning process is such that a manager who becomes knowledgeable in this manner automatically conquers his own self.

This requirement is applicable even more to the CEO positions, because a Chief Executive Officer is in such a leadership position that he can either make or mar the enterprise.

This 'total control of oneself' is necessary in a professional manager for various reasons. Firstly, he has to act invariably in the long-term interest of the organisation he serves. The temptations to take a short-term view of what is good for the organisation are many and strong. Such actions that are in the long-term interest are generally not perceived to be so by many stakeholders. Convincing them within reasonable limits of transparency and democracy is a task that strains all aspects of self-control by the CEO.

Secondly, he has to strongly resist the temptation to act in that kind of self-interest, which is not necessarily in the best interest of the organisation. Even within the framework of ethically sound management, the CEO can cleverly indulge in acts of omission and commission, which promote his self-interest at the expense of the enterprise. These actions may be in terms of earning money or previleges, or in terms of retaining or acquiring power, prestige, etc.

Thirdly, the CEO has to ensure that he does not succumb to undue pressure from peers, juniors (employee unions), and seniors (board members, political heavy weights)towards taking decisions detrimental to the long term interests of the organisation.

Fourthly, the temptation to do good for the organisation at the cost of the society or the nation in general, and to the detriment of the vulnerable stakeholders in particular, is one of the most difficult to avoid. Such measures, especially those that are at the cost of the society, often get approved by those concerned with such decisions in an enterprise, especially if these are not patently illegal.

Lastly, in the tug of war between forces for and against the interest of the organisation, situations can arise where the CEO cannot accept a decision forced upon him against his firm conviction. The only professional alternative is to quit. One must be prepared to abandon the position of power and of status, and be prepared to face the consequences. Such preparedness comes only through total self-control.

Only those who are capable - enriched with worldly knowledge - and also humble - knowing fully well that I alone am not the doer who can guarantee the desired results - will manage to be in control of their selves. In Cāṇakya's view, the so capable naturally becomes self-controlled.

A non-capable, if allowed to rise to or placed at any position of power, will not be able to control their actions towards achieving the organisational goals. His energies will be spent on preserving his position by whatever means, and his decisions will thus not necessarily be in the interest of the organisation.

## 10 जितात्मा सर्वार्थैः संयुज्येत ।

*jitātmā sarva-arthaiḥ saṅyujyeta*

The self-conquered shall endow himself with all resources.

The previous *sūtra* states that the one who has acquired knowledge becomes self-controlled; there is no advice to develop self-control. But in this 10th and the last *Sūtras* of the first chapter of Cāṇakya's teachings on management, he advises the student-manager to acquire, to get hold of as many different resources as he can: resources of money, materials, skills and men. It is only with these resources that he can hope to accomplish the desired tasks successfully.

Significant in this entire process of management education as envisaged by Cāṇakya is this fact: no advice whatsoever about acquiring resources is profferred until one has conquered oneself i.e. won control over the 6 enemies of reason. Only the mature professional, who has acquired the worldly knowledge from elders through humbleness, and who has internalised it so as to make it a part of his normal behaviour, is expected to start acquiring and using resources.

The process of acquiring resources does not automatically follow after one has mastered oneself. This has to be a deliberate action taken towards the task of building up an enterprise. Hence, this specific advice to the mature students - those would-be managers/ rulers.

We thus see that Cāṇakya's thinking on Management is distinctly different from the modern concepts formulated in the West, mostly after the World War II; i.e. in the second half of the 20th Century.

What is the next step after conquering oneself and equipping oneself with requisite skills and capabilities? That is told in the next chapter on 'Counsellors'.

### *Sūtra* Summary: Foundations

May wealth and glory that you/the students of management - will generate, protect you all.

Happiness for all is through ethical behaviour, which in turn rests on possessing adequate resources generated through enterprise. Only by acquiring the knowledge of the world after getting trained to control the organs of sense and action, by humbly serving those elder in knowledge and wisdom, can one possess the necessary worldly wisdom leading to total self control. After conquering oneself should one go after acquiring as many resources as possible.

# CHAPTER 2 ॥ मन्त्रिणः ॥ Counsellors

1 अर्थसंपत् प्रकृतिसंपदं करोति ।

*artha-saṁpat prakṛti-sampadaṁ karoti*

Wealth of resources leads to wealth for the people

*Saṁpad* stands for abundance, and excellence, besides for wealth. Abundance of wealth is an advantage. The constituents of *prakṛti* are - the chief, the officials, the country, the castles, the treasury, the army and the allies. All these can reach levels of excellence given abundant resources. In the present context, we may interpret *prakṛti* as meaning employees, stakeholders such as vendors (allies) and people of the society (the conventional meaning).

Why should one strive to acquire resources as told in the last *sūtra*?

We get two clear messages here. One, the abundance of resources that the manager has at his disposal makes it possible for him to offer benefits to others: this wealth of resources is meant to be shared with the employees who work for the goals of the enterprise. Two, those resources should be shared with the stakeholders, including the people in the society in general; both in an equitable way, based on ethical considerations. The process of creating wealth amongst employees and society through wealth generation is the enterprise. It is important to note that having advised a competent and self-controlled individual to acquire resources and wealth, the very next *sūtra* tells him the reason behind it - not for self gratification alone, but for sharing with the employees – colleagues and with the people in society in general.

If the resources are not shared / distributed with a sense of fairness, the consequences will be bad to the organisation, and consequently also to the manager himself, in the long run. This truth was clearly understood by Cāṇakya, who goes on to state the inevitable and good consequences of equitable distribution of resources amongst the people.

2 प्रकृतिसंपदा अनायकं अपि राज्यं नीयते ।

*prakṛti-sampadā a-nāyakaṁ api rajyaṁ nīyate*

Through excellence/abundance of people resources (the officials, the army, the allies, and the subjects), is led an enterprise even without a chief.

When the distribution of wages and salaries is not fair and just amongst employees; and with whom power (another resource) is also not suitably shared in a systematic way, the internal politics in an organisation will be unhealthy. The pulls by those who feel deprived, and the pushes by those unduly and undeservedly put in possession of resources, together lead to manipulative and unscrupulous politics, resulting in disturbances of all kinds. In the present circumstances, the power of the labour or staff unions would get used very negatively if a sense of fairness is not perceived. Even when fairness exists in the perception of the management, it may not be so perceived by the labour unions or by the staff. Even the people around, in the society, hold perceptions about the fairness (ethics) of such enterprise to its employees and to the society (In the case of a kingdom or a state, this phenomenon is naturally very evident).

On the other hand, when the people in general and the employees in particular feel satisfied about the distribution of resources, the organisation functions smoothly. Satisfied with the ethical distribution of money and powers, each employee would be willing to put in his good work to fulfil the role assigned to him in the organisation. Little or no supervision would then be needed to ensure that employees at all levels of hierarchy do their assigned work properly. Therefore, Cāṇakya mentions that the organisation will function well even without a chief executive officer, when resources are shared equitably with employees and society. Was the meaning of the word probity in terms of employees and the society really meant by Cāṇakya here? Was he really aware of the role the employees and the society can play in the continued existence of an enterprise?

## 3 प्रकृतिकोपः सर्वकोपेभ्यो गरीयान् ।

*prakṛti-kopaḥ sarva-kopebhyo gariyan*

People's anger is the greatest of all angers

Here is a strong warning: the anger of the employees (and officials or managers, the army, the allies) and also of the society in general is the most to be feared, because it is the worst anger that one can invoke or that happens to get generated when actions are taken without a serious thought to their short and long term consequences. Such anger of the employees is generated because of unfair distribution of resources and unfair use of power.

If the CEO takes actions which anger his senior managers or supervisors, it is certainly bad. But if the actions cause anguish and anger to the large labour force (the people of an organisation), it is worst. Again, experienced managers need not be reminded that such disturbances are the largest when issues relate to distribution of money, or to use of power in an unjust way.

Do the people in the society get disturbed and angry even when the enterprise management is possibly fair to the employees? In the case of a government, such a question is obviously answered in the affirmative, and that is implied in Cāṇakya's statement. However, given a democratic political system and a market economy, the wrath of the people against an industrial unit is not only possible but can also be very destructive to the business enterprise. Several examples of these can be seen on the international business scene as well as on the Indian scene after the market reforms were ushered in. In this context, too, one sees the relevance of the very first *Sūtra* – the basis for happiness is ethics.

4 अविनीतस्वामिलाभात् अस्वामिलाभः श्रेयान् ।

*a-vinīta-svāmi-lābhāt a-svāmi-lābhaḥ śreyān*

Not having a chief is preferable to having a chief without humility/morality.

After stating that the anger of the people is to be avoided, Cāṇakya says that the people or the employees should prefer not having a chief to having an arrogant one without scruples. Such an untrained and undisciplined person in position of power would take actions to satisfy his ego and to fulfil his own desires, at the expense of the good of his employees or of the people of his society. This would lead to a great anger which in turn would lead to a rebellion by the people or to a mutiny by his own employees.

The word used – *svāmi* means an owner/master/lord or sovereign. Any group of people, when it desires to accomplish something, usually looks for a leader amongst themselves. A leader is manifest through his superior capabilities such as his knowledge and skills; and his willingness to exert himself for the common goal. Such a leader is either selected by common acceptance or gets elected by consensus. Very often, the leadership position comes to a person through heredity and people are expected to honour this position. Irrespective of the way in which a group of people happen to get a leader, Cāṇakya says that the leader better be a non-arrogant and morally right, trained and self-disciplined person. If he happens to be otherwise, better to move away from under such chief as an individual or to get rid of the chief by acting as a group; and to make do without one, till another good person can be found.

## 5 संपाद्य आत्मानम् अन्विच्छेत् सहायवान् ।

*saṁpādya ātmānaṁ anvichhet sahāyavan*

After equipping oneself, seek helper(s).

Immediately after the *sūtra* advising that one should enrich oneself with resources (1.10)*, the next four *sūtra* are general statements on distribution of resources and response of people to resource sharing and leadership. Only after this is made clear, does

---

* 1.10 donotes chapter 1, *sutra* 10.

Cāṇakya advise his students to look for another person to help him. It is not simple to select the right person for help. Often, the tendency of an individual would be to go ahead by himself, to avoid problems that may arise from seeking help of one or more persons. The verb form used for seeking, also means longing for, desiring and selecting. The emphasis is on strongly desiring for and then selecting the right kind of persons for help. Why should one not function alone? Especially a capable person who has also learned to control himself well? Many a managers, especially senior executives, have the strong tendency to 'go alone'. Cāṇakya literally forbids it. The main reason is given in the next *sūtra*.

## 6 न असाहयस्य मंत्रनिश्चयः ।

*na a-sahāyasya mantra-niścayaḥ*

No certainty in policy for one without help.

The word *mantra* has several meanings: counsel, consultation, plan, and policy are relevant in management thinking (The commonly understood meaning of '*mantra*' is a secret set of words repeated as incantation, usually for good spiritual purposes or even for bad black magic purposes. Obviously, this meaning is non-relevant in the context of management of an enterprise or a kingdom). The word *niścaya* can mean ascertainment, firm conviction, certainty or definite conclusion – i.e. deciding upon with certainty: all these make good sense here.

The student - the would be manager – is emphatically told that when one thinks on his own and makes a work plan or formulates a policy, he cannot be sure of its being effective. Everyone of us who has done many things in life in a planned manner realises that an individual often thinks in a manner convenient to his purpose, either too optimistically or too pessimistically. The planner – policy maker manager – tends to ignore, even unknown to himself, several factors which can impinge upon the proposed policy or work plan. If the plan is talked over with someone else, the chances are much better that new, unforeseen facts or possibilities will be discovered. Consequently, the plan can be modified to suit all the facts, and possibilities, rather than basing it on only those thought of by the first person alone.

Knowing the strong tendency of the capable individual to plan or decide upon policies by himself, the next *sūtra* gives an apt metaphor to dissuade this student – manager from such action.

## 7 न एकं चक्रं भ्रामयति ।

*na ekaṁ cakraṁ bhrāmayati*

One wheel cannot make (a cart) roll.

Just as a chariot or a cart needs two wheels to roll smoothly when pulled by a horse or a bullock, so is it necessary to have at least two persons to work together to get good results. Not that a single wheel cannot roll at all: one can visualise a chariot with a single wheel. It would roll forward certainly, but will not be able to keep to the desired course and will be very difficult to control. The journey would take unexpected turns and twists, and the likelyhood of collapse would be much higher. Therefore, this major emphasis on selecting helper(s).

8 सहायः समसुखदुःखः ।

*sahāyaḥ sama-sukha-duḥkhah*

Helper is the one who has identical happiness and unhappiness.

This advice on 'whom to select for helping oneself" is interestingly, very different from our normal reactions: we go to a friend or to someone with who we are comfortable in consulting. Cāṇakya warns his student manager to carefully consider who else will be in the same position as himself when circumstances change. Will the things that give you happiness are the same things which give the possible helper also happiness? Similarly, will those things which cause unhappiness to you also cause him unhappiness? If yes, then consider this other person for helping you in your task, otherwise, do not. If he is likely to benefit/be happy when things go bad for you or vice-versa, he is not the right person to help you decide plans and policies for future actions. In other words, Cāṇakya advises neither to look for the right or similar attitudes nor for similarity in status or compatibility in temperament etc. while selecting a helper. He wants the manager to ensure that only a person with the same long term interests as his own is selected to work with. When two such persons work together, it is always a 'Win-Win' situation for both simultaneously; and no conflicts of interests will arise even in future. Obviously, capability of giving the kind of assistance that is needed, in terms of knowledge and skill, is implied.

This advise on whom to work with or with whom to collaborate as an enterprise is borne out of considerable experience and astute observations. A gem of management thinking found rarely elsewhere.

9 मानी प्रतिमानिनम् आत्मनि द्वितीयं मन्त्रम् उत्पादयेत् ।

*māni prati-māninaṁ ātmani dvitīyaṁ mantraṁ utpādayet*

One entitled to respect should generate within himself a second plan/policy as if done by his opposite (respect worthy) person.

Even after saying that you need some one else to consult with for deciding upon your plans, the advice given is to think through yourselves about what someone who may not be so involved with your plan or someone who might want your plan not to succeed would develop his own plan. This is like playing chess: you decide your moves after considering the counter moves of the opponent. Also after thinking of what others like you could have done in your place.

A second plan – an alternative plan – must also be generated and compared with the first that has occurred to the manager. This is the equivalent of the present advice that a manager must develop several alternatives before he acts. This is easier said than done. We know that one gets obsessed with the first complete plan, and one gets more and more convinced that it will work. To develop a meaningfully different alternative plan takes quite some self-discipline and training. Such self-discipline, which goes along with humility, helps the manager to listen carefully to those who have been selected to help him. Those who simply agree are not true helpers at all in ensuring that the plan or the policy achieves the desired result.

10 अविनीतं स्नेहमात्रेण न मन्त्रे कुर्वीत ।

*avinītaṁ snehamātreṇ na mantre kurvīta*

Do not seek advice from/consult with an arrogant/morally untrained (person) only because of friendship.

Keep friendship and consultation separate. Do not confide (this is one meaning of *mantre kuru*) with a friend about your plans simply because he is a friend . You may do so only if the friend deserves to be consulted because of his capability in terms of humility, self discipline and moral rectitude. If he does not have it, search for another. Especially if this friend of your has a big ego and is not particular about being ethical, keep him away from consultation even if he is your friend.

The kind of person, besides being endowed with humility and moral strength, that one should consult is stated in the next *sūtra*.

11 श्रुतवन्तम् उपधाशुद्धम् मंत्रिणम् कुर्वीत ।

*śrutavantaṁ upadhā-śuddhaṁ mantriṇaṁ kurvīta*

Make him a minister who is learned (and) who has passed the integrity tests.

Neither the word *śrutavān* nor the word *upadhāśuddha* have equivalent words in English. Learning is acquired through 'listening' what elders/wise and peers/juniors say: and quite some part of knowledge giving was done earlier by the spoken word from the Gurus and from the scriptures. Those who have learned well by this method – rather than acquiring just bookish knowledge – were known as *śrutavān*: those who have learned by listening. We may denote them as 'listening-learned': the worldly wise through experience amongst people (The other, more common meaning of *śrutavān* is learned in the vedic knowledge': this was applicable in Cāṇakya's time since the duties of *varṇa* and *aśrama* were based on vedas).

*'Upadhā'* is in fact a procedure to test the incurruptibility of an employee. This procedure consisted of putting the employee (to be tested) in charge of a job where he can make a little money 'on the side' or 'under the table' for himself (obviously, either at the cost of the state/enterprise or of the party seeking to get some job done through the employee). If he does not get tempted, good. Then put him on another job which can 'yield' somewhat larger gains to him illegally. If still not tempted, put him in yet another position where the unlawful gain is very large. If he still does not get tempted, conclude he has good integrity as far as 'money' goes. Tests were similarly done for temptation to other strong human desires – wine, women, power position, advantage to relatives/friends etc. – and also to religious convictions. The appointed official *(amātya)* was tested through temptations from money, desires and religious convictions and fear – *artha, kāma, dharma,* and *bhaya.* Depending upon which kind of temptations the employee can withstand, he was employed in an appropriate position. (In his treatise 'Arthaśāstra, Cāṇakya gives illustrations of how to tempt, and then advises where to employ such integrity tested persons. He says that only those who have been proven to withstand all four types of temptations be given the ministership by the king). The word *śuddha* means innocent, guitless, cleared, acquitted. An employee cleared through the four types of integrity tests and found to be incurruptible should be deployed as a minister or used as a counsellor. Those who fail on all counts should be used not as officials, but as workers at the lower rungs

of hierarchy, under controlled supervision.

This *sūtra* recognises the worldly reality that even an accomplished person is prey to temptations of unethical behaviour, which goes towards gratifying his own needs by non-permissible means. Cāṇakya certainly knew that many a person can be bought at a price and the price can be in different forms. Therefore, this advice for 'testing on the job' for integrity. The advice for employing such high-integrity , honest persons can be given only by those who are themselves totally honest and ethical, and have set the right example through their own behaviour. The leader – the top managers - have to be the right kind of role models to others. We now see the importance of earlier *sūtra* on 'conquest of organs' (*indriyajayaḥ*) and 'conquering own self' (*jitātmā*). These are pre-requisites for being able to get help from capable people with unpierceable integrity.

How to proceed after seeking help from the right type of counsellors? That comes in the next chapter on policies/strategies.

### *Sūtra* Summary: Counsellors

Wealth generation - in terms of money resources and power - leads to wealth to employees and to the society. Where such wealth is equitably shared, an enterprise can perform well even without a leader or a chief. The anger of people is the greatest of all angers: therefore, better have no chief than to have one without humility and moral rectitude.

After acquiring resources, look for help from those who become happy or unhappy with the same events as you would be. Without help neither plan nor policies can be confidently developed; just as one wheel cannot make a chariot to roll well. Even so, generate alternative plans/policies within yourself the way your adversary or an independent colleague will think through.

Do not consult an arrogant/non-ethical person just for the sake of friendship. Select as counsellor a worldly-wise person tested and found to be of high integrity in terms of money, desires, religious conviction, and fear.

# CHAPTER 3 ॥ मन्त्राः ॥ Policies/Strategies

1 मंत्रमूलाः सर्वारम्भाः ।

*mantra-mūlaḥ sarva-ārambhāḥ*

All beginnings are policy/project based

Cāṇakya now begins to use the word *mantra* in a specific technical sense. As mentioned in the introduction, one of the important words which is used by Cāṇakya in a technical sense is *mantra*. Common language meaning in this context of management would be consultation or policy. In Arthaśāstra, Kautilya (i.e. Cāṇakya) states:

"कर्मणाम् आरम्भोपायः पुरुषद्रव्यसंपद् देशकालविभागौ विनिपातप्रतीकारः कार्यसिद्धिः इति पंचांगो मन्त्रः ।"

"The five parts of *mantra* are: method for starting the work; (planning for) men and material resources; (determination of) place and timing; (means of) overcoming difficulties that can arise; and accomplishment of work."

Clearly, Cāṇakya has used the word *mantra* to mean the total process of work planning and implementation. Neither of the words 'consultation' or 'policy' convey this meaning of a 'process': converting them to 'consulting' or 'policy making' would bring in the sense of a process at work. A more appropriate word would be 'project planning', which would stand for a process as well as indicate different steps involved in planning and implementation of work towards maximising the probability of its successful accomplishment. Just as the process of *mantra* can be carried out entirely by an individual acting by himself, so can strategising be done by an individual singly. 'Cosulting' does not lend itself to such usage, though policy formulation does. In deciding upon any policy a manager does consider the five aspects mentioned above. So, policy making can be considered to be a category of the *mantra* process defined by Cāṇakya: a category applicable to work items which occur repeatedly while managing an enterprise. We will therefore use the word 'project' for '*mantra*'.

Unless these five aspects of any specific work are thought through, discussed with colleagues, and then crystalised for action, that work should not be started. Policies occupy a large and important place in the process of *mantra*, but leave quite some space for many other work items which are essentially non-repetitive. In fact, as experienced managers would agree, many of the work items which are vital to the survival and growth of an enterprise are non-repetitive. Therefore, in this chapter on *mantra*, we will first look at 'policy making' for repetitive work items and then 'project planning' for non-repetitive work items. Expectedly, many considerations will be commonly applicable to both.

Cāṇakya has most probably not used the word *mantra* in the sense of policy. However, all these *sūtras* on *mantra* fit well for this interpretation also. It is therefore worthwhile to look at the implications of both meanings of *mantra*: namely, policy and project.

a) **Policy**

As every administrator knows, any action can and often does, set a precedence. This makes it easier to take similar actions in future, irrespective of whether the initial action is good for the organisation or bad for it. Similarly, every manager knows that taking any action which appears to be ad-hoc, has several unintended consequences. Different concerned or even unconcerned persons – amongst the employees or from the society – interpret this action in their own way. They – all human beings, indeed - are conditioned by their past experience and attitudes. They interpret the action by attributing motives to it: motives which cover a wide spectrum: from the charitable and the good at one end to the devious and the bad at the other end of the spectrum, with all mixed hues in between. For both these reasons of administration and management, the strong advice is: "Begin every single new action on the basis of a policy". When you think of any type of action for the first time, do not act until you take steps towards policy formulation. In other words make a three step plan,

1. Think through the possible interpretations and consequences of any new (of the kind not taken earlier) first action, and formulate a new policy. This policy will help you to decide specifically which similar actions needed now or to be taken in future will be considered appropriate and consistent with this policy.

2. Also think of the nature of actions which will be considered inconsistent or contrary to the policy.

3. Finalise the new policy first and then take the first new action under that new policy.

This process is advised to ensure that a manager does not ever act in haste, which would invariably induce many unexpected and unwanted consequences. When every new action is based on a policy – and the policy has to be sound or robust – the likelyhood of success (getting the desired result without adverse 'side-effects') becomes higher.

The manager – the CEO especially – has to guard himself especially against taking apparently 'good' actions – good for employees, work at hand etc. to which no one objects or where – in the short term – no disadvantage is seen.

The philosopher-Poet-King Bhartṛhari has a good verse on how to take actions in general, and this verse is also applicable to management.

गुणवदगुणवद्वा कुर्वता कार्यमादौ । परिणतिरवधार्या यत्नतः पण्डितेन ।
अतिरभसकृतानाम् कर्मणामाविपत्ते । र्भवति हृदयदाही शल्यतुल्यो विपाकः ।

"Before taking any action, whether virtuous or otherwise, the wise must make efforts to anticipate its consequences. Those who act in great haste, beget a heart burning consequence like an arrow in the body – after the result of action turns out to be adverse".

Note that this warning is also for undertaking a virtuous action. A manager has to guard against the 'temptation' to take a 'good action' in haste, for the adverse consequence can be not only to his heart, but also do the good of his enterprise. And, of course, besides thinking of consequences, he needs to fit his action in a policy framework, as Cāṇakya specified. After all, Bhartṛhari's advice is to the common man, while Cāṇakya is a Management Guru.

b) **Project**

Non-repetitive tasks do not need any policy framework, but nevertheless they need to be thoroughly planned even before starting them. Small or big, whether marginal or large in impact, each new task must undergo the five-fold process of project planning.

The 'method for beginning' would need to address issues such as selection of a leader, whether to undertake a preliminary survey/analysis of feasibility and benefits, how to announce start of work and to whom, and several others of similar kind. The next group of questions would relate to the kind and number of men to be deployed for the task, the monetary provisions, the provision of right kind material resources to be available in time etc. The third part of this five-fold project planning process is perhaps the most difficult to manage: namely, the decisions on when and where to start and to execute the task. Managers often discover a little too late that 'the time was not ripe' for successful accomplishment of work, or that it would have succeeded if tried out 'elsewhere' in the organisation. Essentially, the place and time judgements are subjective, based upon an intuitive evaluation or assessment of a multitude of factors that can affect the course of any new work started in the organisation. Personal judgements about individual persons and their interactions, about the effect of events on individuals and groups etc. are all involved in such decision-making. The risks of mis-judgement, especially for an over confident, arrogant and power conscious – *avinita* –

manager, are very high. Therefore, Cāṇakya has included this twin aspect of place and time for a formal analysis in his *mantra* process. The very fact of 3-4 persons considering these aspects of work in advance would help considerably in ensuring that a right decision – one more likely to lead to success – is taken. But this is not enough, according to Cāṇakya. His fourth element consists of anticipating the different kinds of difficulties or obstacles that can arise, and thinking of actions for overcoming them. The word used is *vinipāt*, whereby *nipāt* indicates an happenstance which occurs as a side effect without having planned for it, and the pre-fix *vi* indicates the adverse effect of the happenstance on work accomplishment (sometimes, such happenstances can also have beneficial effects, and the work gets accomplished faster and better than planned. Such 'good' side effects need not be, and should not be, thought of while planning a work, since that would lead to inefficient planning). The fifth aspect of 'successful work accomplishment' is somewhat surprising at the first glance: what is to be planned in advance when the task is successfully completed? But as all top executives know, every completed work has several ramifications. Will the success be sustainable in the long run? Will some person or group feel threatened by this success, either in real term of their power/authority etc. or in their not so valid perception of the changed circumstances? What kind of next steps need to be taken and by whom? How best to exploit the changed situation towards faster growth of the organisation or towards improved work satisfaction of employees? Many such questions arise and need to be answered formally and in advance.

2 मन्त्ररक्षणे कार्यसिद्धिः भवति ।

*mantra-rakṣaṇe kārya-siddhiḥ bhavati*

Protecting policy/project plan leads to work accomplishment.

a) **Policy**
Taken as a sequel to the previous discussion, we can understand this statement as self-evident. Herewith, Cāṇakya has given the specific reason why all new actions must be based on policy. If you want your actions and your work to be successful then giving them a policy base is a must. Experienced administrators and managers will be able to recall quite a few examples from their own experience of how a policy framework leads to success and how ad-hoc actions lead to unexpected and unwanted consequences, often leading to disturbances in the work atmosphere and in lowering of quality and productivity at work.

b) **Project**
Adhering to the planned strategy leads to success, if any team member were to think of something else than planned and do it, the consequences can be troublesome. Since the other persons on the same job would not know of such impromptu deviations from the plan, they would continue to follow the planned course, creating unexpected difficulties. Obviously, between any plan and its execution, there would arise unexpected circumstances. This has been taken into account in the fourth aspect of the strategising process of *mantra*; but even this may not suffice. This *sūtra* emphasises that the temptation to take an unplanned decision without further consultation amongst the team members is to be avoided.

Being based on a good policy or on a well thought out project plan is a necessary condition for success of any action, but not a sufficient condition. As we have noted earlier in our commentary, the 'doer' does not have control on the 'result', because of the Fifth Element of 'chance'. This aspect will get covered directly by several *sūtras* in Chapters 11 and 12.

## 3 मंत्रविस्रावी कार्यं नाशयति ।

*mantra-visrāvī kāryaṁ nāśayati*

One who lets policy/project plan trickle away, causes the work to be unsuccessful.

This statement is complementary to the previous one: it states the negative consequences of not following the established policies. Even after a manager has been told that protecting the policy or the project plan while taking actions leads to success in tasks undertaken, why is it necessary to make this additional statement? Cāṇakya is aware of the temptations to which a manager is subjected to take a quick action which looks OK, or sometimes to feel that a small borderline exception to the policy/ deviation from the strategy may not cause any trouble. It is to warn the manager against yielding to such impulses that a negative statement has to be also made. Here, the 'destruction of work' or failure is almost certain; but again, not guaranteed because of the Fifth Element of 'Chance'!

## 4 प्रमादात् द्विषतां वशम् उपयास्यति ।

*pramādat dviṣatāṁ vaśaṁ upa-yāsati*

Owing to inattention or mistakes (the managers) get pushed

under the influence/control of adversaries/enemies.

The first *sūtra* on consequence of non-protection of policy and project plans was about the success at work; the second *sūtra* talks about the political consequences to the manager making such error.

a) **Policy**

Not only does the action not succeed when laid out policy/strategy is or happens to get flouted by any action, but such action also leads to a very undesired and harmful consequence. Every organisation has its own not so benign politics: every manager (person in position of even a little power) has others who are jealous of his success/position/popularity/acceptance from seniors and peers etc. There exist also adversaries who wish to usurp his position or at least show him up in poor light. One little policy mistake or deviation, and they will take it up in a big way to bring pressure on the manager who has failed. Instances of management being caught and pressurised in a bad way by labour or staff unions by catching them on the wrong foot abound in all industrialised countries. Such reactions of adversaries were more virulent in the mixed-economy of India because of over protection of the 'rights' of the 'labour'. In a competitive market economy, even the labour and staff become aware of the danger to the business in terms of its survival and would normally not take up small policy deviations for creating any major disturbance to the business process.

It is to prevent such a bad consequence on the position of the manager that no deviation should be made from a laid out policy. When the credibility of the manager gets affected adversely or eventually gets destroyed through even inadvertent policy lapses, he is no more able to exercise his authority effectively to get the organisational tasks accomplished. He loses his freedom to act in the best interest of the organisation and he has to compromise by taking decision under the influence of adversaries, who are more interested in their own advantage, even at the cost of the enterprise or business itself.

b) **Project**

Mistakes can take place or unilateral deviation from the plan developed through consensus can occur in any of the five aspects of the project planning process: in the method of beginning, in timing or in place, or in the actions to be taken to overcome possible difficulties, and even after the work is accomplished, in the manner in which the next steps are to be taken. Mistakes can also take place by way of changes made in the person to be employed for the planned job element, or in making available the right resources. Each of these kinds of deviations from the planned strategy will have adverse consequences of political kind, besides decreasing the probability of successful accomplishment of the task.

As distinct from policy deviations, the adverse political outcome of such mistakes is amongst the work team itself, rather than spread over the entire organisation. If one member deviates, others would also be tempted to take similar liberties. Mutual trust can get destroyed and the adverserial members or other work teams can start exercising their influence in a way that is not conducive for success.

Cāṇakya, an experienced manager himself, brings out this adverse consequence of faulting on policy/project plan in a succinct and fully generalised way. Even managers who have lived through several such instances and their consequences would find it very difficult to derive and to state such a generalised principle.

## 5 सर्वद्वारेभ्यः मन्त्राः रक्षितव्य ।

*sarva-dvārebhyaḥ mantraḥ rakśitavyaḥ*

Policy/project plan must be protected from all doors (loopholes/leakages).

a) **Policy**

There exist too many doors – exits, ways out, holes, loopholes – through which a policy may trickle away or get defaulted. Policy defaults can occur knowingly or unknowingly, intentionally or unintentionally, through acts of omission or commission or through any combination of all such factors. This, the manager is made aware of, and is told to guard against. Many a managers know that policies made in a hurry, without taking the necessary precautions, cannot be maintained over the long term. This is because several situations arise which require making exceptions, in order to take effective decisions. Therefore, this *sūtra* also conveys that if you want to protect the policy you make from the fate of dissipation, better start with a well thought out policy. Even good policies lapse, because they are not adhered to consistently, and employees clearly perceive this to be so. Then they draw their own conclusion that this particular policy is only on paper or is implemented only when convenient to the management or the manager. Thereafter, the policy loses its meaning because most will not bother about it. So, do not take any new actions without policy, and once made, adhere strictly to that policy. If a policy is seen to be un-meaningful or is seen to lead to unexpected and undesired actions, it is better to carefully amend the policy and then to protect it.

b) **Project**

When any new work assignment is being planned, ensuring confidentiality of the proceedings is crucial. Any 'leakage' of information about any one of the five aspects of project planning can lead to others – both within the organisation and outside – using it for their own purposes. Leakages invariably lead to extra difficulties in carrying out the work and inevitably reduce the chances of successful completion. Cāṇakya goes to the extent of saying, "Even birds (parrots!) can hear and reproduce parts of the consultative proceedings, not just the servants or bearers etc. who keep coming in for service". Prior information – even hints or indications – obtained by adversaries on timing, on place or about the expected difficulties and their counter-actions can prove disastrous to the success of the task.

## 6 मन्त्रसंपदा राज्यम् वर्धते ।

*mantra-saṁpadā rājyaṁ vardhate*

Wealth of policies/excellence in projects makes the enterprise grow (thrive/prosper).

a) **Policy**

A large set of policies, naturally consistent with each other, is meant here under the word *'mantra-saṁpad'* – wealth of policies. It is through the means of this wealth of policies that an enterprise can be made to grow. We know that when an organisation has developed a good set of policies to take care of all aspects of work, the work gets done smoothly i.e. without undue interpersonal friction, and without undue delays.

Differences of opinion would always exist, and should not be discouraged. But a meaningful resolution of differences is needed for taking a consensus decision which will be acceptable to all, and which will be supported by all. Such resolution of differences is facilitated when one has a set of policies available to guide in the right direction. The chances of success for the work taken up in this manner are obviously much higher then otherwise. In the case of decisions not truly accepted by all concerned, a sabotage of intentional or unintentional kind, through acts of commission or omission, is very likely to take place, reducing the probability of success considerably.

b) **Project**

In the context of project planning as the meaning of *mantra*, the word *sampad* stands for excellence. When the consultative, consensus building process of project planning involving the five important aspects is carried out well, almost all tasks undertaken will succeed. The enterprise, therefore, will grow consistently. This statement draws attention of the manager to the fact that these management meetings on project formulation should not be taken as a 'ritual' to be gone through. Only if their *mantra* process is genuine, i.e. conducted with full involvement and with creative application of mind by all participants, will it lead to success work assignments, consistently. Another way of using this *sūtra* is to look at the results over a period of time. If the non-successes are several, and or growth does not occur, one must critically re-examine the consultative process being followed, detect lacunae and improve to reach excellence.

Thus, it makes good management sense to state that a wealth of policies and excellence in projects management helps an enterprise to grow. That this was perceived so clearly and expressed explicitly about 2300 years ago is a remarkable fact indeed!

## 7 श्रेष्ठतमाम् मंत्रगुप्तिम् आहुः ।

*śreṣṭhatamāṁ mantra-guptiṁ ahuḥ*

Pre-eminent amongst means of protection is said to be the policy ; OR
Confidentiality of project plans is said to be the most important.

This is the only *sūtra* where Cāṇakya uses the word *āhuhu* – meaning, "it is said" (by others, who are expected to be knowledgeable). It is, therefore, not clear whether he agrees with this statement. As mentioned earlier, in his treatise Arthaśāstra, Cāṇakya refers to others' opinions alright, but invariably states his own view justified with reasons for selection. This word has been used to state the fact that in general, policy is considered to be an excellent means of protection. This general observation by knowledgeable persons is given in support his own *sūtra* on sets of policies and their usefulness.

The word *gupti* means preserving, protecting or a means of protection, and also concealing or hiding. The policy is, thus, also a means for protection of the enterprise from disturbances, mainly from within the organisation. Confidentiality of strategic plans is vital.

Cāṇakya uses a double-superlative *śreṣtha-tama* to praise policy protection, policy as a means of protection, and keeping strategies confidential for the enterprise, which needs to survive over a long period of time.

## 8 कार्यान्धस्य प्रदीपः मन्त्रः ।

*karya-andhasya pradīpaḥ mantraḥ*

For a workblind, policy/project plan is the lantern.

a) **Policy**

A person perplexed about what to do-what action to take – is a workblind; he does not see his way to effective action. Policy, at such times, serves like a lantern. It shows the way to act. When in doubt about whether to take one action or the other, or when quite foggy about what to do next, the policy guidelines help the manager to decide wisely. A manager needs to take effective actions: actions which produce the desired result with a high probability, and which are likely to produce undesired consequences with a low probability. Without a policy to guide him he can be really in a blind spot. He would not be in a position to discern or to asses what the results of his actions can be. Using an established policy, or, if necessary, developing a new policy for use, will help him to take more effective actions. So, one more reason for setting down policies is given here, and one more use of policies is indicated.

b) **Project**

The use of 'project plan' as a lantern for the work-blind is two fold. When the task on which a manager is engaged has already been strategised earlier, he can refer to the various planned alternative actions and the type of discussions that went into crystalising them. This kind of back reference will help him to decide upon the right action to take.

If the situation is new, the manager would do well to call for a new *mantra*, rather than to rush into any action by himself.

There is yet another important use of policy, and project planning as stated in the next *sūtra*.

9 मन्त्रचक्षुषा परच्छिद्राणि अवलोकयन्ति ।

*mantra-cakṣuṣa para-cchidrāṇi avalokayanti*

Vulnerable spots of other(s) are observed/detected using the policy/project planning as eyes.

a) **Policy**

Continuing the simile of blindness and vision, policy is now seen as vision. One important use to which a set of policies should be put is to discover lacunae in the systems of work. No work system can be perfect, the manager's aim should be to keep moving towards the idea of perfection by removing or by resolving mechanisms or misfits that he comes across. Policies help us to locate such vulnerable spots and to take suitable corrective actions to eliminate them.

Similarly, policies should be used to observe and to evaluate the behaviour of colleagues, juniors, or even seniors. Any one who tends to deviate from or disregard policies, needs to be given corrective feedback.

If vulnerable spots are left unattended, they can develop into fostering sores which later on break out or erupt to cause a disturbance in the entire body organisation. To illustrate, a few lacunae in the recruitment or in the promotion policies within an organisation can lead to a 'wrong' person being put in a position which can do severe damage to the organisation. And in these times of organised and unionised labour or staff, putting a wrong person in even a lower hierarchical level can prove to be a great nuisance (We are not referring to the legitimate needs or desires for which the unions have a right to fight for, and should have, in a democratic market economy. The need for organised labour/ staff, in such an economy is accepted and welcomed, for various reasons. In an advanced market economy, unionised employees are aware of the need for survival of the enterprise, which acts as an automatic check on their destructive behaviour).

Management should possess the humility to listen to criticism on their policies from all levels of employees. Their perceptions on policy implementation may or may not be valid, but are important in either case. Non-valid perceptions need to be removed through good communication, and the corresponding adverse consequences avoided. Valid perceptions should be used for improving policies, giving due credit to those who speak up.

b) **Project**

The five elements of the process of project planning - *mantra* - are used also for detecting vulnerabilities of different kinds, including those of the persons involved in execution.

When discussing on how to begin, which material resources and which individuals to employ for the work assignment, the possible lacunae get revealed. The process of anticipating different kinds of difficulties is in fact a search for vulnerabilities from all angles.

Another reason for stating this *sūtra* is to tell the top management to use the *mantra* process deliberately for detecting weak spots - the chinks in the armour being made by the management.

## 10 मन्त्रकाले मत्सरः न कर्तव्यः ।

*mantra-kāle matsaraḥ na kartavyaḥ*

At the time of (formulating) policy/project plan, jealousy ought not (be allowed to) operate.

After establishing the need for policies, the management Guru now proceeds to inunciate the general principles of 'how to develop' good policies and how to ensure excellence in strategising. His first statement is a strong admonition against letting petty jealousies, or strife with others, or hate for any individual or any group to become a basis for policy making. Hate or jealousy should not be allowed to affect the process of policy making. No policy making or consultation should take place when *matsara* is present: i.e. envy, jealousy, hostility, enmity, pride, greediness, anger, passion is present. No policy should be either directed against or set for any particular individual or group. A policy or strategy is meant to be a guideline for the organisation to function smoothly, and therefore, person based emotions (especially negative emotions) must be kept aside while formulating every single policy and when planning any new task to be taken up.

Experienced managers are aware of the temptation at the senior levels to formulate 'convenient' policies to give legitimacy to their proposed actions against or in favour of some individual, group or event(s). Even intelligent and otherwise capable managers are seen to let their negative emotions influence their thinking while developing work project plans in groups, consciously or sub-consciously. Such situations must be avoided in the interest of achieving the organisational goals. A manager ought not to indulge in any kind of *'matsara'* while formulating policies or planning projects . Here is one more reason why a manager needs to have conquered himself (*jitātmā*) first, before assuming a managerial role.

## 11 त्रयाणम् एकवाक्ये संप्रत्ययः ।

*trayāṇaṁ eka-vākye saṁpratyayaḥ*

Firm conviction (validity) through concurrence of three

In the last chapter (2.6) was the advise that plans or policies cannot be developed without help of at least one more person. When it is a question of laying down policies, two are not enough: three are minimum needed. Which three are meant here? It appears that the three concerned persons should be the CEO, his second-in-command (SIC) and the head of the department most concerned with the contents of the policy to be laid down. A reference to the text of Arthaṣastra shows that Cāanakya has discussed mainly the 'number of persons' to conclude on 3, or at the most 4, as optimum. He refers to the disadvantages of 'time needed to reach consensus decision and difficulty in maintaining confidentiality' as reasons for not exceeding this number 4 i.e. the CEO plus at the most 3. If situation demands, he says even 8-10 persons may form such a decision group.

This observation of Cāṇakya is rather significant. Even after saying that personal biases should be kept aside while formulating any policy, he advises that only two persons should not be doing the job of developing policies. Apparently, he was aware of the tendencies of the SIC to be agreeing with the views of the boss. The SIC may do it genuinely out of respect for his boss's wisdom experienced by him in the past, or he might do it for out of political prudence or out of diffidence in his own different point of view, or even simply owing to psychophancy. The SIC may even sincerely have the same point of view quite independently of the CEO. But in any of these situations, a worthwhile second view is not available for discussion. When a third person, also knowledgeable and likely to be directly affected by the policy is present, he is most likely to express his point of view candidly. The need of this third person to show his capability vis-a-vis SIC also helps this process. This would normally prompt even the SIC to come out with his own different views. And the CEO, who should have formulated his own alternative policy for the proposed one 'within himself' (2.9), can also become a 'devil's advocate'. A healthy discussion would follow, various consequences thought off, alternatives wieghed, and a consensus arrived at on the exact nature and the scope (and the wording) of the policy. Only such a policy can be considered as convincingly effective or valid - i.e. meaningful for an organisation to abide by for taking effective actions towards reaching the specific goals for which the policy is being made.

Identical considerations apply to the process of developing project work plans in their 5 distinct aspects.

12 कार्याकार्यतत्वार्थदर्शिनः मन्त्रिणः ।

> *kārya-akārya-tattva-artha-darśinaḥ mantriṇaḥ*
>
> Counsellers (are those) who show which action to take or not to take by citing meaningful principles.

Policies are to be developed not by oneself, but with the help of at least two more counsellers or managers. What capability should these managers posses to be able to do a good job? Their qualifications have been specified earlier (ch.II, 11) as learned through listening (wordly wise) and tested for integrity. Their skill or ability is being specified here. These managers (counsellors) should be those capable of advising the CEO what is worth doing and what is not worth doing. Typically, any one can give this type of advice and, in reality, every one gives such advice! In fact, each manager – especially the CEO – gets such advice even without having asked for it!! The CEO gets it from juniors as well as seniors, and also from the press and other members of society. Therefore, willingness to give ideas on what to do or not to do is not a criterion, nor is the ability to think of different ideas for this. A true counsellor should be able to reason out on the basis of appropriate and applicable principles, and, thereafter, show why it logically follows to take a specific course of action (which includes 'no action', too).

When a manager seeks advice from superiors, it may be given to him with a quiet not-to-be questioned authority. When a peer or a colleague is asked, the tendency will be to look at the advice favourably or otherwise depending on relationships built earlier.

When advice is offered by juniors, even when asked, predisposition will be to give less importance to it than it deserves. All these kinds of responses are likely to occur even when just three (and certainly if more) persons set out to lay down a policy or to strategise a task. Hence this advice from the experienced management Guru Cāṇakya: let every one involved, and each of them is a counsellor in his own right, give his views on what needs to be done on the basis of principles. Once it is ensured that good, mutually consistent principles are followed, the policies or project plans that get so developed will be very sound and will be more likely to be widely acceptable. Consequently, these policies would form a set which will make the enterprise grow and reach unprecedented heights.

## 13 षट्कर्णात् भिद्यते मन्त्रः ।

*ṣat-karṇāt bhidyate mantraḥ*

A policy becomes discriminating from hearing by 'six ears'
or
A project plan gets divulged when heard by 'six ears'.

The verb *bhid* stands for about 14 different meanings – the common usage is of the meaning "to break, cut asunder, rend, or pierce". Since '*mantra*' commonly means a secret mumbo-jumbo, this *sūtra* gets thoroughly misinterpreted in the context of management principles. This verb also means to expand, to cause to blossom, and to disclose, to divulge. Given the previous *sūtra* on "three are needed for the validity," the appropriate meanings of *bhid* are of two kinds. In the context of policy, these are 'to discriminate and to expand or to cause to blossom'. In the context of strategy, these are 'to disclose or to divulge, or to break'.

Heard by three persons – six ears – the policy becomes discriminating, it distinguishes itself.

The word *ṣaṭ-karṇa* is commonly used to refer to 'ears of unauthorised persons or outsiders to the task group' etc. In this context, any leakage of strategised plans to outsiders will lead to the project being 'broken', leading to failure.

This final *sūtra* on policy and project planning emphasises the process of policy formulation by at least three persons, and also the confidentiality of the deliberations involved in formulating strategies.

### *Sūtra* Summary: Policy/Project Planning

All beginnings (new actions or tasks) should be based on policy (for repetitive items) or project (for non-repetitive work). Protecting policies/projects leads to successful work accomplishment. The one who lets actions deviate from policy/ project plan makes the work fail. Mistakes in adhering to policy/ project plan pushes the manager under the influence of adversaries/those who hate him. Therefore, policies/project plans must be protected from all sides.

Set of well-laid policies, excellence in project planning helps the organisation grow. Policies are called the best means of protection. Keeping confidential all project plans is considered of upmost importance.

Jealousy or such negative emotions must be kept away while formulating policies or projects. When three (counsellers) agree, the policy/project is sound. Consellors are those who show 'what to do and what not to do' on the basis of meaningful principles. A policy becomes discriminating when heard by three persons. A project plan gets destroyed if leaked to outsiders.

CHAPTER

# 4 ॥ राज्यतंत्रम् ॥ Management

1 आपत्सु स्नेहसंयुक्तं मित्रं ।

*āpatsu sneha-saṁyuktaṁ mitraṁ*

Friend is one who stays with you with affection during adversity.

After talking about helpers and of counsellors, Cāṇakya turns to friends. Here again, the definition of a friend is 'A friend in need, is a friend indeed'. And not समानशीलव्यसनेषु सख्यम्— i.e. friendship is between similar characters or between those in similar danger or difficulty. The emphasis given by Cāṇakya is on affection or goodwill between friends during difficult times. Here, no skills or knowledge is being specified. This is somewhat similar to the *sahāyah* or helper, where again the same happiness-unhappiness was the criterion; not skills. When it comes to counsellors, both qualifications and skills become important and therefore, necessary.

The manager should carefully study and use this definition of a friend; many show friendliness when they have something to gain, but drop all pretence of friendship when they themselves need to give help.

2 मित्रसंग्रहणे बलं संपाद्यते ।

*mitra-sangrahaṇe balaṁ saṁpādyate*

In obtaining friends, strength is achieved.

The use of the seventh case (in, within) in preference to the third case (by or through or by means of) for the noun *'sangrahaṇam'* (collecting, bringing together, getting) is to be noted. The idea is to convey that making friendship with many and to have a large number of true friends is a strength by itself. It is, therefore, worth striving for making a good group of friends who will stand with you even in times of trouble, difficulties or danger. This kind of strength is vital for taking further steps towards building of an enterprise.

3 बलवान् अलब्धलाभे प्रयतते ।

*balavān a-labdha-lābhe pra-yatate*

The strong exerts himself for obtaining that which is not possessed (by him).

It is only the strong who will make attempts to get what he wishes to posses, to acquire, to gain. The weak would find almost everything which he desires to be beyond his capacity to achieve; consequently the weak may not even attempt to procure what he wishes for. The strong does put in such efforts. What we need to note is that this person – this would be manager – is strong according to Cāṇakya because of several accomplishments. These are: (1) conquering of organs (2) acquiring humility and moral strength (3) becoming worldly wise (4) conquering of self (5) choosing a helper (6) choosing counsellors (7) learning about importance of policies and how to develop them and lastly (8) forming a group of friends. This is quite some list, but apparently, something more is also needed, as we see from the next *sūtra*.

## 4 अलब्धलाभः न अलसस्य ।

*a-labdha-lābhaḥ na alasasya*

Gaining that which not in possession is not for the lazy.

No gains whatever can come to the lazy, he would not put in the necessary efforts to get things done. Why is such an obvious statement being made at all? Those who wish to accomplish any major task need to put in continuous efforts: not just a sprint of strong efforts over a short duration of time. Energy of the kind needed to persevere over a long period, and not to relax when small successes are obtained, or not to give up efforts when difficulties loom large, is not easy to come by. Moreover, when a manager finds himself in a comfortable position of doing well by most counts, the natural tendency is to take things easy. This also is laziness of another kind. It is for this reason that Cāṇakya stresses on diligence or industriousness in a negative manner by telling the manager "do not be lazy' if you want anything to be gained".

Who are the persons who can become accomplished as listed under 3 above? Only from that economic class where these 'gentlemen' have the liesure enough to spend time on such activities as learning. Earning money for daily upkeep of themselves and their families is not their problem. Even the accomplished individuals of such well-to-do class can turn out to be lethargic or un-enthused for perseveringly hard work. Laziness does not hurt them at all in the short term. All the more reason to emphasise that such laziness will not help them gain anything.

5 अलसस्य लब्धम् अपि रक्षितुं न शक्यते ।

*alasasya labdhaṁ api rakṣituṁ na śakyate*

The lazy cannot even protect that which is gained.

The laziness or the lack of application or commitment that comes to any person who does not need to earn his livelihood, almost invariably would lead to his losing what was given to him. A person who has spent efforts in gaining something worthwhile, relaxes after such gain. Complacency after gains is a general human experience – a rather common failing.

When a person becomes complacent, he relaxes on the vigil that is needed to conserve the gained, to not eat into the principal and live only on the interest, to take efforts to protect the gained from pilferage or outright theft by others. Efforts have to be continuous and of appropriate kind to be able to preserve that which has been gained earlier by the manager either by his own efforts or by efforts of his predecessors or forefathers. Those who are lazy by attitude and by behaviour, cannot manage even to protect the gains, leave aside gaining something on their own.

6 न च अलसस्य रक्षितं विवर्धते ।

*na ca alasasya rakṣitaṁ vivaradhate*

Neither does the lazy person's protected (gains) grow.

Complacency of an attitudinally lazy person leads him to be satisfied with whatever he already has or what he has already gained earlier. He would not make efforts to make his gained and protected to grow. Nothing that has been 'gained and protected' will stay so unless efforts are put in to make it grow. Maintaining 'status quo' is a good looking goal or objective, but circumstances continually change and only a downward slide can take place when efforts are made to maintain status quo. To emphasise the need for growth, the verb form is not just *vardhate* but *vi-vardhate*: where the pre-fix *vi* refers to distinction and intensity.

## 7 न भृत्यान् प्रेषयति ।

*na bhṛtyān preṣayati*

(The lazy) does not deploy employees (servants).

A lazy person is one who does not feel the urge or who does not possess the enthusiasm to put in efforts of any kind. If we think that a lazy person is the one who gets other people to do his work for him that is also not really correct. A lazy person lets things happen to him, or for him; he lets others work for him. The other people do what they themselves want to do, including things which are helpful to the interests of the lazy person. A manager, on the other hand, requires that other people under and around him work for the same goal which he and his organisation have set for themselves. To accomplish this goal, he has firstly to judge, then to select them for placing in appropriate positions, to direct them to do specific tasks over specified time periods, and to monitor their performance by results. This is what is meant by deployment of employees. Such deployment takes lots of efforts, which a lazy or not really motivated person will not take. How can this lazy person then acquire new possession, protect them, and make them grow?

8 अलब्धलाभादि चतुष्टयं राज्यतंत्रम् ।

*a-labdha-lābhādi catuṣṭayaṁ rājya-trantraṁ*

These four, starting from gaining the non-possessed, together constitute the technology of enterprise (management).

Now, after as many as 40 *sūtras,* we come to the definition of management in this collection of aphorisms on excellence in management. The beginning is with statements about human society, then the turn is towards the individual manager, and the need for accumulating resources, and acquiring skills, thereafter come the counsellors and the policy development process. It is only after this that gathering friends to become strong to be able to run an enterprises is talked about. This system for running of an enterprise or the administration of a kingdom, or the management of an organisation consists of only four elements.

1. gaining possession of non-possessed
2. protecting that which is gained
3. making the protected grow
4. through deployment of employees

Here we find a very simple, and yet elegant, definition of what constitutes management. It is also easy to understand and to remember. We may compare this definition with that found the modern (20th century onwards) books on management – the books that are used in the management schools all over the world. Although no single definition seems to have been universally agreed upon, the commonly accepted versions include five elements that constitute management: planning, analysing, organising, coordinating, and controlling or monitoring.

The basic difference between these two definitions is obvious: the modern definition refers to the processes involved in management, while Cāṇakya's definition focuses on the purpose of the whole business of management. A manager is the one who analyses, plans, organises coordinates, controls etc. etc.: so what? What does he do it for? How to measure the effectiveness of this type of management? The moment one wishes to evaluate or to assess the 'quality' of management, one needs criteria or measures external to this definition. We need to look at some result(s) of the process of management. One can think of many 'results' as measures of effectiveness: speed of action, satisfaction of employees, happiness of society and, of course, also the profitability of the enterprise. The modern definition of management is, by its very nature, neutral to any of these measures. A situation can, therefore, arise where a wonderfully well managed organisation which keeps everyone satisfied may end up making losses, and ultimately cease to exist!

Cāṇakya's definition of management, on the other hand, has the measures of effectiveness of management built into the definition. The definition is of objectives of management, and the processes to be used are left out of this definition. A management is good only to the extent if fulfils three, easily measurable, expectations:

1. gaining that which is not possessed
2. protecting whatever is gained
3. making the protected grow

This is an ENTREPRENEURIAL DEFINITION of management, not an MANAGERIAL (or ADMINISTRATIVE) definition of management. The entrepreneurial spirit of creating wealth is the very first stance. Retaining the created wealth, managing it well, is the next part. But most interesting is the thrid part – make the wealth grow continuously. Why does one need to keep on growing in any business? Why not be satisfied with protecting and preserving over a long time whatever one has gained already? In the present day industrial world, where market economy is the norm, it is a common experience that a business survives in the long run, only when it makes efforts to keep growing. It can grow only if it adapts itself to changing external circumstances, and thus manages to satisfy the changed needs of those whom the enterprise serves. It is indeed remarkable that Cāṇakya had perceived this principle and had incorporated it right in his definition of *rājya-tantra* – the technology of running a kingdom – i.e. of managing an enterprise. That this is not a happenstance or chance becomes clear as we proceed further along the *sūtra* path of teaching/learning management. In Chapter 9 we will see a strong statement saying that "being satisfied with wealth/ resources causes the wealth/resources to dissipate". (9.6)

The fourth part of the definition, of course, is integral to management or administration of an enterprise or a kingdom. Managing through other persons is the only way to undertake any really major enterprise for creating wealth. The verb *'preṣayati'* is important – it means deployment – placement of the right person at the right job. That this meaning is implied while using this verb becomes certain when we find a specific *sūtra* stating this in Chapter 12. (12.2)

Here is a definition of management which every manager in any market economy must remember every day of his work: what has he contributed today to creating, maintaining or growing wealth? The bottomline-contribution to profits or the gains – is the most important, perhaps the only, criterion of judging whether he as a manager has been worth being paid as an employee. It is unimportant whether you plan or coordinate or monitor well – you performance is to be judged not by the process but by the result. Cāṇakya knew this well. No wonder he was the first management Guru of the world to define management thus. He trained Candragupta and his friends to ultimately take over the Nanda dynasty and to run it well.

### *Sūtra* Summary: Management

Friends are those who retain affection during adversities. Collecting friends begets strength. The strong one exerts to win what is not in his posession. Such gains are not for the non-industrious (lazy). The lazy cannot even protect what is gained. Nor does the protected grow for the lazy. He does not deploy employees.

Gaining the not-possessed, protecting the gained, making the protected grow, through deployment of persons constitutes management.

# CHAPTER 5 ॥ राज्यनीतिः ॥ Management Science

1 राज्यतंत्रायत्तम् नीतिशास्त्रम् ।

*rājya-tantra-āyattaṁ nīti-śāstraṁ*

Science of ethics/politics depends upon the technology of enterprise (management).

The word *'nīti'* has several meanings; and so has the word *'śastra'*; the combined word *nītiśastra* means political science, science of ethics and science of morality. These meanings convey a reference to the political situation in the enterprise (kingdom) and the ethical, moral and legal behaviour of the employees. This is governed, literally determined, by the methodology or the technique of management. If the king's own systems involving his ministers use improper means to obtain gains, it is futile to expect that his other employees and the subjects of the kingdom to be abiding by good ethical and moral practices. Even authorised legal codes of conduct are unlikely to be adhered to under such circumstances.

The same is the case in managing an enterprise in market economy. If the top management is seen to adopt all kinds of means to manage the system i.e. its own actions are seen to be violating business ethics, the senior management cadre as well as all other employees will feel justified in breaking or bending the internal rules and the external laws for their own benefit. Such undue benefits may either be direct gains to the employee or a gain to the enterprise which would later result in a gain to the concerned employee.

Cāṇakya's statement is clear: following business ethics is the job of the top management who 'call the shots' on 'how an enterprise is managed'.

## 2 राज्यतन्त्रेषु आयत्तौ तंत्रावापौ ।

*rājya-tantreṣu āyattau tantra-āvapau*

Home and foreign relationships depend upon enterprise management.

Since Cāṇakya's *sūtras* are meant to guide rulers of kingdoms, he naturally talks about the two major aspects. Managing within the kingdom and simultaneously, safeguarding the position of the kingdom in the context of the world outside the kingdom. He mentions here the work areas of the Home Ministry, and of the Ministry of External Affairs. As mentioned in the introduction, not each of the *sūtras* written in this context is likely to be meaningful when we apply it to management of enterprises. However, as we do know, one of the tasks of top management is to ensure a 'good fit' of their organisation with the (ever-changing) business environment. So, it is possible that several of the *sūtras* on 'External Affairs', would prove meaningful in business context also.

The term '*tantra*' has several meanings in different contexts. As we note, the word *tantra* comes along with *rājya* to talk of management technique or technology or system or method or science. Therefore, Cāṇakya proceeds to specify in the next two *sūtras*, what he means by the words *tantra* and *āvapa* here.

Interestingly, this is the first time, and one of the few times, that Cāṇakya uses this methodology of 'defining' technical terms – jargon - in successive *sūtras* (This well-known *sūtra* technique of successive definitions has been used very effectively by Patanjali[9], when he laid down the principles and processes of Yoga. Clearly, he was using so many commonly used words in a technical context, that he must have felt the need to define and to describe his terms in specific technical manner. Apparently, Cāṇakya has rarely found the need to do so).

In the previous *sūtra* on *nīti-śastra,* Cāṇakya forms a joint word out of 'management and dependance', while in this *sūtra,* he uses the seventh case of the word *rājya-tantra* to refer to internal and external affairs. This difference in forms signifies that while *nītiśastra* depends upon management, internal and external affairs constitute two aspects of management, which of course are dependant upon management.

3 तन्त्रम् स्वविषयकृत्येषु आयत्तम् ।

*tantraṁ sva-viṣaya-kṛtyeṣu āyattaṁ*

Actions to be taken (work to be done) in the context of own areas/departments/subjects constitute Internal Management.

The word *tantra* is defined by saying that this term refers to all actions which are within the domain of the enterprise. Actions which refer to law and order, tax collection etc. within the kingdom. Actions which refer to employee related policies, to systems of accounting and of managing production/service etc. within the enterprise. The other implication of the use of the verb form (participle) *āyatta* is that the internal affairs are governed or fully controlled by the top management.

4 आवापः मंडलनिविष्टः ।

*āvāpaḥ maṇḍala-niviṣṭaḥ*

External affairs rest with the surroundings/neighbourhood.

The participle *ayatta* is dropped. It was appropriate in the context of legal/moral order, and of internal affairs because it indicates dependance to a great extent: when it comes to external affairs, this cannot be so. The participle used is '*niviṣta*', meaning is seated in/is dependant on, but neither controlled nor governed by the '*manḍal*'. In political context, *manḍal* stands for the circle of near and far kingdoms which surround one's own kingdom.

In the context of any business organisation – whether 'for profit' or 'not-for-profit' kind, or whether from the manufacturing/production sector or from the service sector – these external affairs are those which pertain to the stake holders outside the organisation and also to the competing organisations. The outsider stakeholders are the suppliers, the banks, the local/state/federal governments etc. and, of course, the society as a whole. The competitors are the other businesses in the same product/range or in other products/services which can replace your products or services cost effectively. Obviously, Cāṇakya could not possibly have referred to these kinds of stakeholders: he implied only competition of the same class, as is evident from the next few *sūtra*.

5 सन्धिविग्रहयोः निर्मण्डलः ।

*sandhi-vigrahayoḥ nir-maṇḍalaḥ*

Through treaty and war become free from (the bad effects of) surrounding competitors.

For regulating the impact of (external factors such as) competition, the right steps are either to 'join them' – *sandhi* or treaty or 'to beat them' – *vigraha* or war. Basically, we can talk about 'M&A' – mergers and acquisitions, even joint ventures in this context. We will find a few *sūtras* later about whom to join with or not attempt to join and also on whom to fight with, in terms of principles.

6 नीतिशास्त्रानुगः राजा ।

*nīti-śāstra-anugaḥ rājā*

The one who follows the science of ethics/politics/morality is the chief.

Who is the chief? The CEO is the one who practices ethics. This is a very peculiar 'definition' of a CEO! Cāṇakya has already stated that the science of ethics/morality/legality is controlled by, decided upon by the technology of enterprise i.e. by the management. He could have thereafter, said that "the chief ought to adhere to principles of ethics and morality." But no: he does not advise what the chief should do: he simply states that the one who adheres to these principles of ethics and morals is the chief. If a person who is in the position of the chief does not so behave, he is unlikely to last as a chief. A no-chief situation will be found preferable (2.4), to be soon replaced by a chief who follows the right practices.

The word *'rājan'* as king or chief, is derived from the verb *'ranjan'* meaning 'taking care of' or 'looking after' etc. The one who has to look after the welfare of all others has of necessity to be ethical in behaviour. Any deviation from morality disturbs the situation and leads to non-fair management of welfare of the people.

7 अनन्तरप्रकृतिः शत्रुः ।

*an-antara-prakṛtiḥ śatruḥ*

The neighbouring souverign (kingdom) is enemy.

Typically, an (neighbouring king) enterprise in the same field of operation, will be looking for vulnerable spots in the functioning of one's enterprise. These competitors would always be keen to exploit such vulnerabilities to their own advantage. Therefore, all these must be considered as adversaries or enemies. One must not only guard against any strike or one-upmanship from them, but also take strategic steps to be ahead of them in terms of internal strength and external relations.

8 एकान्तरितं मित्रम् इष्यते ।

*eka-antaritaṁ mitraṁ iṣyate*

The one who is separated by one is desired as a friend.

The next but one neighbouring kingdom, which is in a similar situation with the direct neighbouring kingdom, should be chosen as a friend, should be requested to be a friend. This is because his and our own interests are common with reference to the middle kingdom.

While this logic makes sense in a geographical system, any corresponding interpretation in terms of a business enterprise does not appear to be meaningful.

9 हेतुतः शत्रुमित्रे भविष्यतः ।

*hetutaḥ śatru-mitre bhaviṣyataḥ*

Enemy and friend are formed with logical reasons.

Neither friendship nor enmity between businesses/enterprises happens to be without a purpose. The word *hetu* has several meanings: cause, reason, object, motive, logical reason, logical point or argument, a means or an instrument; source or origin, too! Almost all make sense in the context of why friendships and adversary relationships get built amongst enterprises (kingdoms, states, nations).

The pragmatism here is worth noting. No reference to ethical or moral principles is seen here. Neither moral considerations nor emotions of positive or negative type should even be the basis of relationships with other enterprises.

Networking, interactions or linkages etc. that are spoken of in modern management books are all meant to have the specific objective or motive of 'gaining something' for our own enterprise from the relationship. In any friendship or enmity between individuals, emotions are expected to play an important role, and such a role for emotions is appropriate. The tendency of individuals to carry such emotions into relationships between enterprises has to be curbed. Only logical reasons and motives of self-interests – and no emotions at all – should be the basis for friendship-collaboration or enmity-competition, or adverse relationship.

What kind of relationships, and with whom is dealt with in the next chapter.

## *Sūtra* Summary: Management Science

Ethics and politics are dependent upon management. In management rest the internal and external relationships. Internal management consists of actions within the enterprise while external management depends on environment/surroundings. Through joining or competing with others, overcome environment.

One who adheres to the science of ethics and politics is the chief. Those in similar business are competitors; a competitor's adversary is desired as a friend. Friends and adversaries (in business) become so with reason(s).

CHAPTER 6

# ॥ सन्धिः ॥
# Alliances

1 हीयमानः सन्धिम् कुर्वीत ।

*hīyamānaḥ sandhiṁ kurvīta*

The weak (on the decline) should seek treaty (collaboration).

After defining friendship and enmity, a set of rules is given to decide what type of external actions should be taken to 'protect that which is gained'.

One should identify one's weaknesses in specific terms and then collaborate – with written agreements signed, like a treaty – with someone else. The emphasis is here on not depending upon one's own self with any wishful thinking of being able to manage on one's own. This directive also shows that even the 'arrogance' of being self-sufficient should not come in the way of a detached realistic appraisal of one's own weaknesses.

This is, perhaps, Cāṇakya's version of SWOT analysis: strength, weaknesses, opportunities and threats. Here, he advocates using an external opportunity to overcome internal weaknesses.

The information available on 'others' can be biased: it needs to be validated. A considerable detachment - looking at own enterprise from an outsider's point of view – is called for to be able to conduct a meaningful SWOT analysis. This is more so when it comes to identifying weaknesses. Only a CEO who has 'conquered himself' can be good at this task.

2 हीयमानेन न सन्धिम् कुर्वीत ।

*hīyamānen na sandhiṁ kurvīta*

(One) should not collaborate with the weak.

With whom should we seek collaboration? Not with another weakling or one on the decline! Why this obvious advice? Both *sūtras,* the previous and this, have implicit in them a careful study of one's own organisation in the context of the environment (Later, in Chapter 11, we will be told more of this) and an equally careful study of the enterprise with whom you would want to (and you should avoid going to) collaborate to protect, and later to improve, your position. Using words like 'weakness' or 'strength' is easy: to be able to truly identify such entities in own and other organisations requires quite some overall understanding and skill.

Various methods of cross-checking, including information specifically collected through spies need to be used to confirm any inference or diagnosis.

3 तेजो हि सन्धानहेतुः तदर्थानाम् ।

*tejaḥ hi sandhāna-hetuḥ tad-arthānāṁ*

Capability is the only reason for collaboration between those with similar resources.

The word '*tejas*' has 20 meanings out of which 6-7 are applicable here! It means might or strength, energy/spirit, strength of character, dignity/authority, moral/spiritual power. '*Sandhāna*' means alliance, friendship, peace, joining, supporting amongst 15 meanings. It would be good to interpret this *sūtra* using all these meanings and also the fact that *hetu* stands for reason, objective or aim, as well as means.

Search for collaboration when weak, do not collaborate with another weak: look for an equivalent party with right capabilities to collaborate with. Cāṇakya makes it clear that any collaboration must by only for improving capabilities of both parties which wish to collaborate. Unless the capabilities are complementary, unless both enterprises stand to gain, the collaboration will not take place. Even if it does get managed, it will not be sustained for the time that is needed for both parties to benefit from it. The situation after collaboration has to be win-win for both parties. Such a coming together of two parties needs a lot of energy, strength of character and appropriate maintenance of dignity of each side.

Obviously, this advice from Cāṇakya, given to the rulers of 'not very large' kingdoms in ancient India, is equally valid for business enterprises of all sizes in the present day. All linkages, all business interactions, all collaborations and, of course the major Mergers and Amalgamations follow this basic principle of enhancing mutual capabilities.

4 न अतप्तलोहः लोहेन संधीयते ।

*na- a-tapta-lohaḥ lohen sandhīyate*

Non-heated iron can not be joined with (another piece of) iron.

One more apt metaphor. (Incidentally, the word *loha* stands also for metal in general and for gold). Unless the two parties who wish to collaborate have felt the heat of the outside forces making them vulnerable, they will not collaborate on a sustained basis. If one of them is cool and feels that collaboration is not really needed, even written legal agreements would serve no purpose!

Another way to look at it is that unless both parties to the collaboration make adjustments (iron getting softened by heat), a good joint would not be formed. Since metal work was known in a reasonably advanced form in India even more than two thousand years before Cāṇakya, he would also have meant to convey that a joint formed with both parts of metal made very hot becomes even stronger than the original metal. He may have indicated, by this metaphor, the synergetic effect of collaboration.

## 5 बलवान् हीनेन विगृण्हीयात् ।

*balavān hīnen vi-gruṇhiyāt*

The stronger should specifically take over the weak/deficient.

This advice makes very good sense in the context of kingdom: if a neighbouring kingdom is weak, better acquire it or dominate over it sufficiently to prevent two disagreeable consequences. One, your kingdom is vulnerable through weak neighbour who can be used by an enemy for the purpose of attack. Two, if you do not, your big enemy will annexe it and become stronger. Looking at it from the point of view of an enterprise in market economy, both ideas make equally good sense. If there exists a weak enterprise in your own field, take it over: we are talking of even hostile take-overs. This is the fastest way to grow.

## 6 न ज्यायसा समेन या ।

*na jyāyasā samena yā*

Not with bigger or equal.

Do not attempt to take over or get into fight with any equally strong enterprise and certainly not when it is stronger. The 'Do' was given in the *sūtra* above, while the 'Do Not' is given here to emphasise the 'Do' clearly and to explicitly avoid efforts doomed to failure. In Kalidasa's famous words from Meghadūta (the epic poem 'Cloud Messenger'), के वा नः स्युः परिभवपदं निष्फलारंभयत्नाः । "Who, amongst those who have begun efforts for a (known) fruitless task, has possibly not become the seat of defeat?" To want to win over or to take over equals or bigger enterprises is certainly a fruitless effort to be avoided.

## 7 गजपादयुद्धमिव बलवद्विग्रहः ।

*gaja--pāda-yuddhaṁ-iva balavad-vigrahaḥ*

A clash with stronger is like the fight between (warriors) elephant-mounted and on-foot.

This similie emphasises further the futility of waging a fight with the stronger; the conclusion is foregone. If your are like a soldier on foot fighting another on elephant you are certain to lose. Do not start such a fight, if you are wise.

## 8 आमपात्रम् आमेन सह विनश्यति ।

*āma-pātraṁ āmena saha vinaśyati*

An earthen pot gets destroyed when it hits another earthen pot.

The simile earlier was for the fight with the stronger. This metaphor refers to a fight with equals. Both get destroyed like earthen pots banged together.

When we take *sūtras* 4 to 8, we get a clear picture of what Cāṇakya wants to say on collaborations, on Mergers and Acquisitions! All these similes and metaphors are nice and appropriate; but what should we do?

## 9 अरिप्रयत्नम् अभिसमीक्षेत ।

*ari-prayatnaṁ abhi-samīkṣeta*

Efforts of (actions of) the adversary should be closely examined/considered.

To be able to classify other enterprises in your own field of operation into weaker, equal or strong, we need a lot of data. From data, we cull information; based on information we come to conclusions; the conclusions lead to formulating strategies on collaboration/merger/takeover/amalgamation. The importance of putting in considerable efforts for closely observing the actions and thrusts of others in the field is strongly brought out.

## 10 सन्धाय एकतः वा ।

*sandhāya ekataḥ vā*

For collaboration or even for standing alone (on own).

It is not only for the purpose of collaborating with other competing enterprises that we should learn more about their efforts and actions, but also for being able to survive on our own. Even if we do not wish to take up any efforts towards merger/amalgamation/takeover etc., one better be aware of what the competition is upto and how it can possibly pose a threat to or offer an opportunity for our own enterprise to grow (not just to maintain it at the same level).

11 अमित्रविरोधात् आत्मरक्षाम् आवसेत् ।

*a-mitra-virodhāt ātma-rakṣāṁ āvaset*

From the opposition of non-friends, ensure self-protection from all sides.

Having advised on how to look at external situation and on how to act under different circumstances, Cāṇakya now turns to an area which can be both external and internal. And now the advice turns again to the individual who is the chief.

The word '*śatru*', meaning the enemy – competing business – was used in the previous *sūtra,* but the word used here is 'non-friends: These need not be outright adversaries who have been identified as such and are known to all. They form only a sub-set of the larger set called as 'non-friends'. The 'non-friends' can exist on your own side. Some of them are strong and do not mind being known as non-friends, if they have means to protect their own position. Others who are strong but vulnerable would not show their hand until they feel it is worth the risk. There would also be weak adversaries, jealous of the CEO/manager, who would throw their lot with the non-friends when they appear to succeed in their efforts against the CEO. Hence this strong advice from Cāṇakya to the CEO; work assiduously towards protecting your own position against all kinds of persons who are likely to be your non-friends.

We go back to verify the earlier advice on gathering friends – persons who will continue to be for you, be affectionate to you, when you are in difficult situations. It is only when the CEO has managed to get helpers, who feel happiness/sorrow by the same events as the CEO, gathered friends, and appointed counsellors/

ministers of the right kind, that he can hope to retain his position. Cāṇakya does not let you forget the fact that, even when you are capable and even as your want to do something good for the organisation, you can do all this only if you continue to be in the position of power. Humility and morality are good, and are essential; but so is the position of power. We note that a capable CEO, strong on both the hard technical skills and the soft human skills, does not have to take resort to dirty and unscrupulous steps to survive in his position of power. Highly developed political skills is a pre-requisite for the CEO position. We now see why the emphasis earlier on controlling the organs and conquering the self for becoming a good CEO or even a senior manager. Not to take unethical steps even to protect oneself in a legitimate position of power takes quite some self-control.

The protection is to be managed from all sides, on all fronts. Formulating good policies, adhering to them, not getting caught through a slip on any policy is one area. Not falling prey to any unethical or immoral temptation is another. Several more are pointed out in later *sūtras.*

## 12 द्वयः अपि ईर्ष्यतः द्वैधीभावं कुर्वीत ।

*dvayaḥ api īrṣyataḥ dvaidhi-bhāvaṁ kurvīta*

Even if just two are jealous, create a division between them.

Two individuals or two different groups of individuals, who are envious of your position, may be amongst your non-friends. When this is discovered (through efforts which should be continuously on), the strategy recommended is to create situations where the two cannot, or do not feel like, or see no gain in uniting together against you, the chief who wishes to maintain his power position safe. Keep the two groups separate with appropriate political skills and actions. The same thinking would apply to other enterprises in the same field. If two of them attempt to compete with you, it would be worth ensuring that they do not join hands.

Having spoken about the dos and don'ts to be adapted for making alliances etc. at the enterprise level, Cāṇakya has turned quietly to the individual level at the leadership position. This is typical: all efforts towards building relationships depend heavily upon the individual in the lead position. If this individual changes, the relationships would invariably get disrupted. One more reason why the leader should protect his position from all sides.

After this turn towards the individual, Cāṇakya continues to tell how a person should behave. He gives his views on organisational politics and how to manage it well, for self-interest as well as for the interest of the organisation.

### *Sūtra* Summary: Alliences

The weak should seek collaboration, but not with a weak. Capability is the only reason for alliance between similarly resourced. Non-heated iron cannot be joined. The strong should take over the weak, but not equals or bigger. A fight with the strong is like an infantry soldier fighting an elephant mounted soldier. Two earthen pots destroys themselves when they hit each other.

The efforts of adversaries should be closely examined, whether for alliance or even for going alone. Self-protection from non-friends should be ensured. Even if just two of them are jealous, create a division between them.

CHAPTER 7

# ॥ आचरणम् ॥
# Behaviour

## 1 शक्तिहीनः बलवन्तम् आश्रयेत् ।

*śakti-hīnaḥ balavantaṁ āśrayet*

The one with less strength should take refuge with one with many strengths.

The words '*śakti*' and '*balaṁ*' are synonyms in common parlance, but their use in politics is with specific different meanings. '*Śakti*' is used more as strength of a person as an individual – meaning the capabilities which he acquires and possesses. A commonly understood triad of *śakti* consists of the will (*icchā*), the knowledge (*jnyāna*) and the actions (*kriyā*). For any attempt at any goal to succeed needs all these three aspects of strength. First, the will to put in efforts to reach the desired goal; next, the requisite knowledge and skills to manage the task; and third, the ability to put in efforts in a persevering manner. A person deficient in one would be considered 'without strength'. *Balaṁ* stands for strength of an individual such as *vidyābalaṁ* or even *daiva-balaṁ*: strength which comes through knowledge and strength which comes due to favourable luck (Here, *daivabalam* would also mean backing of God. One can also hope for *tāra-balaṁ*, i.e. astrological strength, which is equivalent to luck, and not worth a separate mention). For a person in position of power, the traditional strengths were of seven kinds: leader, counsellor, nation, castles, treasury, army and friends. Having a capable chief, good counsellor, a large (and united) nation behind you, well defendable castles, full treasury (monetary resources), defence services and friends is indeed equivalent to being strong.

The individual who is not strong enough in terms of will, knowledge or efforts should seek to serve – to join – take refuge – with the one who is stronger in several ways as indicated above. Therein lies his bright future: he stands to be able to reduce his weaknesses and contribute better to the cause.

2 दुर्बलाश्रयः दुःखम् आवहति ।

*durbala-āśrayaḥ duḥkhaṁ āvahati*

Taking refuge with powerless invites sorrow.

This 'do not' comes after the previous 'do' for several reasons: emphasis, easier to get and thus tempting to go to a weak, idealistic thinking of improving the other by joining etc. This explicit statement is to avoid these all. But the statement is not in the form of a 'Do Not' instruction: only the consequence of going to the refuge of the weak is mentioned.

To get into the services of a not-so-strong chief/manager is inviting unhappiness. The word '*dur-bala* can mean 'power-less' or 'unholy-strong'. Even going into service of an unscrupulous, evil-minded chief will also lead to trouble and to consequent unhappiness.

3 अग्निवत् राजानं आश्रयेत् ।

*agnivat rājānaṁ āśrayet*

Take refuge with a chief (king) like with fire.

This simile is interesting – fire is very useful, we cannot live without fire. Fire is needed for cooking food, for protecting from cold etc. So is the king or the chief a necessity for protection and survival. But if we go too close to fire, it hurts. We cannot take fire for granted or ignore it. Same is the situation with the chief (CEO): keeping a respectable distance is good for survival.

## 4 राज्ञः प्रतिकूलं न आचरेत् ।

*rajnyaḥ prati-kūlam na ācaret*

Do not act or behave in opposition to the chief.

Actions need to be taken only after thinking through the consequences they can lead to or invite. Quite often, only the intended and desirable consequences are seen by the doer of the action. But undesired and unintended consequences can be many. These depend on the perception of the action by adversaries and their interpretation of the motive behind the action, among other things. Therefore, this advice by Cāṇakya is not so simple and obvious as it sounds. We are cautioned that actions that we intend to take should to be analysed for their possible consequences through widely different points of views. Critical is to take into account the possible views of your enemies as well as your non-friends, and then to analyse how they can utilise your action for their own benefit. In this way, one should ensure that no action of his can have a consequence which goes against the well-being of his chief, in whose service he wishes to live and to prosper. Let your action be totally free from sabotage – intentional or unintentional, an act of commission or of omission.

5a उद्धतवेषधरः न भवेत् ।

*uddhata-veṣa-dharaḥ na bhavet*

Do not be one who wears loud clothes.

Wearing arrogant clothing attracts undue attention and gets interpreted by other and by the chief in unflattering ways: so, avoid dressing loudly. Here we see a grouping of different *sūtras* on how to behave when in service of a chief. If we see the nature of the advice given here, it is in the context of management. Somehow, this specific *sūtra* and the next appear to be not quite fitting the rest of the *sūtra*. These two are common sayings for individuals. These are not totally out of place, nor do they belong to the set of other ideas in this chapter. Therefore, we will give only the literal meaning of these two *sūtras*, and leave it to the judgement of the individual reader to decide on their merit for being considered as Cāṇakya's advice to managers.
[Incidentally, this directive on clothing does appear in Arthosastra, but the next one does not.]

6a न देवचरितं चरेत् ।

*na deva-caritaṁ caret*

Do not behave like the gods have behaved.

This is a common saying amongst the Hindus. Hinduism is a religion that accepts a multitude of Gods and Goddesses, while accepting that bowing to any 'god' is the same as worshipping any other (like all rivers lead into the same ocean). In the ultimate analysis, the concept of godhood is uniquely defined. However, the Puranas narrate many stories about gods of different kinds. Some of these are downright of the kind which 'good' and 'rightous' individuals should not imitate or follow. Hence this commonly stated advice!

We note that the epics Ramayana and Mahabharata certainly preceded Cāṇakya (by upto 3000 years), though many of the Puranas available at present are likely to have been composed during 400 to 800 AD. But even the 'doings' of 'gods' or 'chiefs' described in these holy epics are not all worthy of emulation!

We need also note that the Jain and Buddhist Jataka stories, many of which also depict the doings of 'gods', were already prevalent (composed 800 BC onwards, before 300 BC) at that time.

But more importantly, the entire set of teachings by Cāṇakya is without any reference whatsoever to any specific God of any religion. In fact, he does not require the 'concept of god' to be a part of his management teaching just as we do not need it today (Those who so wish, may involve such a god-concept to emphasise ethical behaviour. But such use of any faith-based religious systems would invariably lead to undesirable, non-rational and non-justifiable 'moral' edicts also being followed. Many of these moral but ethically neutral edicts can cause a manager to take poor, ineffective decisions).

It would, therefore, be best to ignore these two *sūtra* as good edicts for management, whether in Cāṇakya's period or at present. Two *sūtras* which belong to the thought process of this chapter were found later in the text, and these are given here as the right items for this chapter, with numbers 5 and 6.

## 5 दुर्बलः अपि राजा न अवमन्तव्यः ।

*durbalaḥ api rāja na ava-mantavyaḥ*

Even a weak chief should not be belittled (looked down upon, insulted, not listened to, disobeyed).

Every employee judges every manager above him, and also his peers and juniors. The CEO or the Chief is often expected, idealistically, to be endowed with all capabilities needed for his job. In reality, no chief can be perfect: he will be perceived to be inadequate or weak in some (or several?) aspects. Such perceptions may not all be valid. Given these facts, and the fact that the chief is in a position of power, the sensible advice from Cāṇakya is "better to err on the safer side": "do not, in any way, behave in a way which would be interpreted as belittling the chief." The consequences, even when not visible immediately, can be quite adverse for your own interests. This kind of belittling is usually done 'behind the back' and amongst groups of persons considered friendly to oneself. Even so, these acts of belittling get transmitted to the chief, usually in an exaggerated manner. Therefore, the best policy is to speak only such words and to use only such body language, that when conveyed by anybody, would not be considered as belittling or insulting or demeaning. It must be noted that Cāṇakya does not encourage psychophancy; time and again he has emphasised that 'disagreements' or difference of opinion based on principles is to be welcome by the boss.

6 न अस्ति अग्नौ दौर्बल्यम् ।

*na asti agnau daurbalyaṁ*

In fire, there is no weakness.

This metaphor emphasises the advice given earlier about taking refuge with the chief in the same way as with fire. Fire is never weak, it will invariably hurt if badly dealt with, whether intentionally or otherwise. It is the same with your boss-better be wary and best be aware!

## 7 न व्यसनपरस्य कार्यावाप्तिः ।

*na vyasana-parasya kārya-āvāptiḥ*

Work accomplishment is not for the vice ridden.

After having advised on 'for whom to work and how', starts the advice on some specific negative traits (behavioural patterns) that need to be avoided. The first statement is about vices in general. Those who are ridden with vices of any kind, do not have any grip on themselves. We know that vices are invariably the kind of temptations which are pleasurable, and are, therefore, easy to pickup. They are very difficult to give up, and they gradually increase their hold on the individual who becomes increasingly helpless to control himself. Therefore, this warning: no work will get accomplished properly from the one who is vice ridden.

Vices are of different kinds and are invariably defined in terms of their being able to make persons addicted to them. In any society, which behaviour or act is to be considered as 'wrong' or 'sinful' or 'taboo' is decided on the basis of moral principles. Some of these acts are also ethically 'bad' and fewer still are legally 'banned'. We, as managers, would need to be away from all morally wrong and addictive vices, irrespective of their ethical or legal classification. This is because of the need for acceptability and for non-vulnerability amongst the employees and in the society at large.

8 इन्द्रियवशवर्ती चतुरंगवान् अपि विनश्यति। इन्द्रियवशवर्तिनि न अस्ति कार्याव्याप्तिः।

*indriya-vaśavarti caturangavān api vinaśyati. indriya-vaśavartini nāsti kāryāvyāptiḥ*

One under the influence organs, even if he were to possess fourfold capability will get destroyed (in him is no work accomplishment)

Another way of describing a vice-ridden person is that he is gives in to the corrupting influence of the organs of sense and action (1. 6). All humans get tempted to act in ways which even they themselves may cognitively acknowledge (are aware of) as unethical, or immoral, or illegal. This happens because the individual has not developed a healthy capability of controlling his actions which he knows to be 'bad' (in the above sense of unethical etc.), but which gives him immediate (relatively quickly) pleasure or satisfaction. We need to understand a basic difference between the laws of psychology as a modern science in the West and the practice of psychology developed in the East. The yoga-science of those whom we now call Hindus, the Zen and the Tao systems of Buddhism etc. talk of methods of controlling the mind. This is radically different from 'suppression of desires' which will then go to the 'sub-conscious mind' and give rise to 'disturbed behaviour' later. The one who controls the five organs of sense and the five organs of actions is not suppressing desires in the modern sense. He has learnt through various prescribed methods (e.g. the *Yogasūtras* of Patanjali prescribe study – *abhyāsa* – meaning an effort to be in that state – and detachment – *vairāgya*: so dees Gīta, a part of Mahabharata) how to not permit undesirable impulses to dictate his actions. The actions of such persons are not dictated by the organs: these persons command their organs to perform as they decide.

The word *catur-anga* stands for a four-fold capability, or four distinct aspects of capability in war. These capabilities were: infantry, elephants, horses and camels. The idea is to express that even a person endowed with all strengths for accomplishing the work will still get destroyed inspite of these strengths. In the context of managing an enterprise the four aspects of capability can be subject knowledge, technical skills, human resource skills and political skills. Such skills might also have been meant in this *sūtra*, since the four aspects of war related capabilities are not meaningful here.

Even such capable persons will end up destroying themselves – not just messing up their work – if they are subject to uncontrollable impulses generated through the 10 organs of sense and action taken together.

## 9 न अस्ति कार्यम् द्युतप्रवृत्तस्य ।

*na asti kāryaṁ dyuta-pravṛttasya*

For one addicted to gambling, nothing is doable (worthy of undertaking).

Gambling with dice was a prevalent acceptable sport of the ruling classes (also?) at the time of Cāṇakya. The worst example is to be seen in Mahabharata, where even a good, ethically wise king, Yudhiṣṭhira, loses the entire kingdom (and his wife!) in gambling. Those indulging in gambling do not take up work that they ought to have taken up, leave their work undone or unfinished or shoddily done.

10 मृगयापरस्य धर्मार्थौ विनश्यतः ।

*mṛgayā-parasya dharma-arthau vinaśyataḥ*

Of those addicted to hunting, ethics and resources get ruined.

Gambling can be indulged in by very many in any society, but hunting (wild animals) has been the sport of the ruling classes till very recently. This was an addictive sport, which took the ruler away from his job a little too often, and a little too far away from where he should be. Cāṇakya speaks only of work not done when its gambling; but hunting destroys both ethics and money (resources) according to him. This inappropriate desire – part of the third *puruṣārtha kāma* – pulls down the first two – *dharma* and *artha*.

These four statements (*sūtras* 7, 8, 9, and 10) on the effect of vices on work and on the person himself, even when he is very capable, are extremely important for managers. They are the persons who are in positions of power, where opportunities for indulging in vices are greater, and where the likelyhood of adverse effect appears (in the short term, at least) to be small. Arrogance can breed unabated and lead to immoral and unethical (some times, also illegal) indulgences, with a self-conviction that the likelyhood of public knowledge about these misbehaviours is small; and even if these were to become known, the level of risk involved is minimal. Cāṇakya had witnessed these things happening at several levels starting from the top, in the Nanda Dynasty. So he, like Confucius 200 years earlier in China, advocated ethical practices to rulers. To make that happen in practice, he strongly advocated self control to managers. The mention of three specific vices here is in the context of the times of Cāṇakya: we would need to include all 'addictive' vices of the present age in such a list to make it contemporary.

If the manager cannot manage himself, how can he manage others and his work? Both his work and he himself will get ruined through lack of self-management or through mismanagement of self.

## 11 अर्थेषणा न व्यसनेषु गण्यते ।

*artha-īṣaṇa na vyasaneṣu gaṇyate*

Coveting wealth (resources) is not counted amongst vices.

Going after money and wealth (resources of all kinds) is not considered to be a vice, says Cāṇakya emphatically. This craving, too, is addictive: since more of money gives more power, which in turn spurs a person for more and more money and power. Cāṇakya had to make a non-negative statement on this desire, because it is commonly considered to be bad to go after money. Given Cāṇakya's insistence on ethics and on conquering the self, making more money (generating greater wealth) is certainly a desirable activity as well as a worthwhile goal. It, therefore, cannot be counted as a vice, though it would be seen to be somewhat addictive, and not commonly perceived as 'good'

Yet another reason why this statement had to be made was possibly the apparent conflict between the spiritual and the materialistic. If the goal of life is the fourth *puruṣartha* of *mokṣa* (salvation), what good it is to go after money or wealth? No wonder almost all religions praise 'simple living' and not 'wealthy living'! At the same time, many prayers to the god are for his blessings to get children (sons!), health, prosperity etc. In India, a trader who works for gains or profits, begins his business by writing two words: '*śubha*' and '*lābha*'. *Śubha* means the good way, by ethical means, and *lābha* means gains. The good comes first, then come the gain. Whenever this principle is followed, going after gains all the time is not a vice.

## 12 न कामासक्तस्य कार्यानुष्ठानम् ।

*na kāma-āsaktasya kārya-anuṣṭhanaṁ*

No undertaking/executing/accomplishing of work for one overcome with love or desire (or for the lustful).

One more addiction – craving for and getting into carnal gratifications excessively – has also been one of the 'sports' of persons with power and wealth. The talk here is specifically about men in managerial positions, rather than women. Women ministers or administrative officers were unheard of at Cāṇakya's time, though Queens wielding power might have been happening. Even socio-biologically, the particular advice is mostly for men in power, if we were to apply it today. One is less likely to come across a nymphomaniac amongst women managers!

*Kāmāsakta* also means a person overcome by any strong desire: lust for women is only one kind of strong desire. Even love for a son or a daughter, or a craving to be considered as a 'good' person can cause a person to lose his mental balance at the time of taking decisions. The need for undertaking some actions can escape his notice, the process of conducting the work at hand can suffer, timely and proper accomplishment of work may not take place.

With managers who are sex-addicts, or who are over powered by any specific strong desire, no work will get properly followed up, since his priorities would get set differently. The importance of conquering the organs of the body comes up again in this context.

### *Sūtra* Summary: Behaviour

The weak should seek help from the strong. Taking refuge with the powerless invites sorrow. Behave with a chief like with a fire. Do not behave in opposition to the chief.

The chief, even when weak, should not be belittled, since there exists no weakness in fire.

The vice ridden cannot accomplish work; under the influence of bodily organs even capable persons cannot accomplish work and perish. For, the gambler, no work is doable, while for the addicted to hunting, ethics and resources get destroyed.

Desiring wealth is not a vice. For one engulfed in desires, there no work execution.

CHAPTER 8

# ॥ दण्डः ॥
# Enforcement

1 अग्निदाहात् अपि विशिष्ठं वाकपारुष्यम् ।

*agni-dāhat api viśiṣṭhaṁ vāk-pāruṣyaṁ*

(Habit of using) Too harsh words is even more significant than the burns from fire.

After giving reasons to the manager on why he should avoid vices, Cāṇakya turns towards the managers' next role of getting things done. When instructions given for doing any job work well, that is fine. But if the work does not go as well as expected, the manager needs to pull-up the person(s) who were entrusted with the job. A tendency commonly observed amongst managers is to scold with very harsh words, demeaning the employee. Not surprising: persons in position of power almost invariably become arrogant on one hand, and often feel that unless they are seen and felt as harsh, the employee(s) will not mend his/their ways. Similarly, if anyone is caught breaking rules or committing illegal or immoral acts, the tendency for the manager to lash out at the culprit with harsh words is common. Moreover, the temptation to show the 'smaller man' his 'low place' is strong.

Cāṇakya does not directly advise the manager not to use harsh words: he draws the managers' attention to an observation he had culled from his experience. Use of harsh words is worse than burning with fire. He uses the word *viśiṣṭa* – significant,.peculiar, distinctive – rather than any word meaning 'harmful'. Not only is the immediate adverse impact severe and painful, but also is the long term consequence: the insult felt by the receiver keeps hurting for very long time, even several years.

Quite often, the manager who utters harsh words on the spur of the moment does not even remember the way they were said. Later, in case he gets a feedback from the receiver directly or indirectly through another person, he may even get genuinely surprised that his words were so hurtful. That is one kind of peculiarity meant here. The other is the general feeling amongst managers that such harsh words constitute only a mild punishment. Not necessarily so, says Cāṇakya, such punishment can be even more hurtful to the ego of the receiver than monetary or corporal punishments.

## 2 दण्डपारुष्यात् सर्वजनद्वेष्यो भवति ।

*danda-pāruṣyat sarva-jana-dveṣyaḥ bhavati*

Owing to too harsh punishments (the manager) becomes hateworthy by all people.

Again, the way chosen by Cāṇakya is to emphasise the consequences of actions by the manager by stating them as 'laws' which relate cause and effect with a high degree of certainty. Just as harsh words will always hurt over a long time, so will excessive punishment always lead to the person who gives such punishment to become worthy of hate by all. Here, we note that the word used is *dveṣya*, and not *dviṣta* a participle which means hated by all. Not all hateworthy persons get hated by all – some who benefit from his harsh punishments (directly or indirectly) may not hate him. They may fear him and/or admire him for his ruthlessness etc. The word *pāruṣya* indicates excessive harshness – i.e. punishment much more than deserved by the person for committing any specific act deserving punishment. (Later, in Ch.14, this point is taken up specifically 14.6 & 7)

A 'law' of behaviour has now been stated: the choice is with the manager. A prudent manager should be very cautious in exercising his authority so as not to use harsh words or to give unduly greater punishment than considered appropriate by himself, his colleagues, and by the uninvolved employees in general. Most managers have the satisfying experience that agreement on 'what is fair' punishment is quite good amongst employees at all levels of work.

3 अमित्रः दण्डनीत्याम् आयत्तः ।

*a-mitraḥ daṇḍa-nītyāṁ āyattaḥ*

Non-friend is controlled through administration of justice/ science of politics.

Again the word *amitra* – non-friend is used, because enemies are those who are 'in the open' and usually outside the enterprise. The one who is within your own enterprise and who would not necessarily stand by with you during adversities, is a non-friend. Law or rules for behaviour are the means to control such a person. The friends, on the other hand, would normally do the right things and their behaviour would therefore need no control through administration of justice i.e. through law enforcement. Unless we have enforceable rules, which would lead to punishment when violated by any individual employee, the possible bad effects of deliberately bad actions of a non-friend will disturb the system. Such uncontrolled acts would invariably damage one of the three objectives of management – generating, protecting and increasing the wealth. The singular form is used by Cāṇakya for the word 'non-friend' possibly to indicate that only an individual or two would act in this manner. The non-friends are not likely to be very many or to form a group.

Consistency of applying any rule and impartiality in applying it to all employees irrespective of their hierarchical positions, cast, religion, language etc. is important. One major policy – *mantra* – would be "All rules/laws apply uniformly to all employees, starting with the chief, and going down to the sweeper"

'The system of civil and military administration' and 'science of politics' are two other meanings of the word *daṇda-nīti*. These meanings, too, are applicable in this *sūtra* and the following *sūtras* in this chapter, though the comments made are in the context of law enforcement only.

## 4 दण्डनीतिम् अधितिष्ठन् प्रजा संरक्षिता ।

*daṇḍa-nītiṁ adhi-tiṣṭhan praja saṅ-rakṣitā*

Staying with the low enforcement systems, the people are protected.

The word *prakṛti* (2.3) and the word *'praja'* have similar meanings in the context of a kingdom: both are collective nouns used to denote a number of people in a set which is defined as 'those normally residing within the boundary of a country"- the citizens' population. However, when the word to be used in the context of protection by law, praja is the preferred word, not *prakṛti*. Prajā stands for large or small groups/classes of persons as well as for individual persons, who need protection and are so protected by law (When Cāṇakya spoke of *prakṛti-kopaḥ* – the anger of the people in 2.3 the people meant are in large groups or classes; not individuals or even small groups.)

In managing an enterprise, we can use the same meanings for *prakriti* and *prajā*. *Prakṛti* would mean all employees together or one or more unions of workers, staff and even officers. While *prajā* would mean groups or sets – usually small or medium – formed by using different criteria for segregation. Examples are: women, persons from scheduled castes or tribes, from a specific village or a state, speaking one language, age groups, length of service groups etc. Such groups, as well as individual employees irrespective of their demographic profile, need to be protected under the rules and regulations of the organisation, with complete impartiality and consistency without exception. It is only when such is the case that we can say that the manager 'stays with the legal system'. Again, a lot of self-conquering is called for to implement a system impartially, and for ensuring that it is also perceived to be so implemented.

The laws within a company that protect employees are all those policies and rules which are applicable to the human resource development; from recruitment to promotions, punishments for misbehaviour, corruption, embezzlement etc. Even the control of non-friends is a part of the overall job of protecting the employees. Otherwise, all different kind of non-friends can cause large harm to the systems meant to protect the good of all employees.

## 5 दण्डः संपदा योजयति ।

*daṇḍaḥ sampadā yojayati*

Control manages wealth (ensures proper resource allocation).

Control - administration of law - ensures that those who have gained wealth (ethically) will be able to retain it undisturbed by others who may desire to acquire it by force. Law also ensures that those who work towards generating more and more wealth for the society by ethical means beneficial to the society are given due opportunities to do so. The distribution of the gained wealth amongst employees and other stakeholders, including to the society (through a structured taxation) is also done through laws. This important aspect of law as a means to ensure appropriate distribution and deployment of wealth is brought out by this *sūtra*.

If the laws are either not fair or are poorly implemented, the wealth and privileges would get allocated inequitably – some getting more than they deserve, while others getting less than their rightful due. If this happens or is perceived to have happened, the expected protection through laws also fails. Though this may not be visible in the short-term, the adverse effects always surface in the long run. It is no surprise that over 80 per cent of conflicts at workplace in the industry or even in other organisations start from resource allocation systems. These *sūtras* 4 and 5 show the very deep insight that Cāṇakya had gained on affairs of people.

6 दण्डाभावे मन्त्रिवर्गाभावः ।

*daṇḍa-abhāve mantri-varga-abhāvaḥ*

Without control, no ministerial class!
(An alternate version is *tri-varga-abhāvaḥ*)

This is an interesting, but quite unexpected statement. Why should the existence of ministers or counsellors depend upon the existence of a framework for justice? Or is the alternate version 'three classes' more meaningful? The fact that the four *varṇa* system at the time of Cāṇakya was supported through the legal system set up by the king is perhaps being brought out by this alternate version of the *sūtra*. The upper three *varṇas* needed protection, otherwise all would be like *śūdras*, the fourth *varṇa*. But then, the word *varga* should not have been used in place of *varṇa*. Therefore, we conclude that *mantri-vargaḥ* is the right word for this *sūtra*.

When there is no good system for administering justice, and for ensuring that rules and regulations are properly followed, the entire administration becomes chaotic. In such a lose, law-less situation, appointing officials to serve as ministers does not make much sense. Even if these ministers were to be capable managers, their word would not get followed. And when someone fails to do what has been told to, a system to enforce the instructions given is not available to the minister. The situation is as bad as if there were no minister.

Another way in which there will be no ministerial group is that such ministers will not be appointed at all by the king, knowing that such appointments would turn out to be only on paper.

A third way in which this *sūtra* would hold good is that good ministers will leave the kingdom.

All these ideas are applicable to a business enterprise, where the CEO has to ensure good administration of justice. In its absence, good managers will become ineffective, senior posts may be vacant and the good amongst existing managers would leave the organisation.

7 न दण्डात् अकार्याणि कुर्वन्ति ।

*na daṇḍāt a-kāryaṇi kurvanti*

Given law, (people) do not commit deeds which ought not to be done.

Use of law – enforceable rules publicly stated and accepted by a large majority of the employees as fair – is essentially meant only in a negative sense. Laws usually state 'that which should not be done' – theft, forcible acquisition of property, rape etc. in a society. Within an enterprise, laws usually forbid pilferage, embezzlement, sexual harassment, corrupt practices etc. This aspect of law – in fact, the main reason for existence of laws – is expressed succinctly in this *sūtra*. Given good laws and proper enforcement as seen from punishment given to those guilty of breaking them, employees of an organisation avoid doing the wrong things. And these wrong things need not only be 'crimes' – these include the tendencies to do less work, refusing to do a type of work or a specific assignment given by the manager etc.

8 दण्डनीत्याम् आयत्तम् आत्मरक्षणं ।

*daṇḍa-nītyāṁ āyattaṁ ātma-rakṣanaṁ*

In law enforcement lies one's own protection.

This is one truth that most do not understand explicitly. Any power position continues to be so only to the extent that the power is seen to be duly exercised for the purpose for which it is given. It if is not so exercised consistently to enforce rules of behaviour on the employees, they quietly realise that 'the talk is not being walked' in this organisation. Not only does the tendency to ignore the rules and to flout the rules increases, becomes widespread, but also the powers of the manager dissipate. A manager is seen to be either weak, or stupid enough not to notice the rule breaking behaviour. Such a manager will not last. He will either be removed by the higher ups or be thrown out/replaced by a colleague or junior through demonstration of his own capability. Cāṇakya, therefore, expressly states that a manager's position depends on his 'managing' his affairs properly. His protection, too, lies in upholding the laws, the rules, the policies, and ensuring that these are enforced without exception. Politics gets played unavoidably within every organisation; good political skills are needed to protect oneself. Non-vulnerability in terms of rules etc. in own behaviour is a a necessory condition for the survival of a manager.

9 आत्मनि रक्षिते सर्वं रक्षितं भवति ।

*ātmani rakṣite-sarvaṁ rakṣitaṁ bhavati*

In protecting own self, everything becomes protected.

How important is the position of a manager – of a CEO – for reaching the organisational goals and for maintaining a good organic growth of the enterprise? We all know that a good person at the helm makes a world of difference, to the extent that not getting a chief is better than getting a 'bad' chief (2.4). Even so, the CEO – the manager can function only if his position is protected, and when his health is protected. Only when he truly protects himself physically, mentally, and also in terms of his organisational position will everything else get protected. Examples where lack of such care to protect oneself leading to displacement of the manager, and to non-fulfilment of the planned task are many. (Even assassins – political or mafia or terrorists – understand this principle well!).

## 10 आत्मायत्तौ वृद्धिविनाशौ ।

*ātmā-āyattau vṛddhi-vināśau*

Growth and destruction depend on own self.

The emphasis given by Cāṇakya to the manager as an individual culminates in this *sūtra*. Having said in a passive way that the things that should not be done are not done by employees through use of rules, he tells the manager to enforce rules in his own self-interest. This is followed up by saying that unless the manager protects himself, his work cannot get accomplished. And now comes the responsibility and accountability "The buck stops here" at his own self. Clearly, his own growth or decline, as well as the growth or decline of the enterprise the manager runs is in his own hands. No one else, nothing else, no event outside of him can become a reason or an excuse for non-achievement of growth. If a series of uncomfortable events start occurring in the enterprise or to the enterprise in the given (or changing) environment, he must still consider himself as responsible. Of course he cannot control most external or several internal events, but he can certainly find ways to overcome their adverse effects. Some threats can be converted into opportunities, if one faces them with courage and wisdom (Later in 14.9 comes a statement that 'only the immature narrate difficulties at work'. Quite some advice on 'how to accomplish work' is given before that). Only those aspects of growth or decadence which are consequent to enforcement of rules are considered here; and they do form a large part of sustaining an enterprise.

11 दण्डः हि विज्ञाने प्रणीयते ।

*daṇḍaḥ hi vijnyāne pra-nīyate*

Law enforcement/punishment, indeed, is carried into effect through worldly wisdom.

Enforcement of rules – even when these are explicitly and clearly formulated – is not a simple affair. The manager needs considerable judgement and discretion, coupled with an emotional detachment which helps to get the right perspective on the issue at stake. Has the alleged breach or rules really taken place? If so, was it intentional, first time, motivated, part of a large game plan, out of personal distress, pre-meditated or on the spurr of the moment? Several such questions need to be considered and answered realistically, based invariably on insufficient and often contradictory evidence. Even to be certain about the validity of the alleged offence or misconduct takes quite some judgement. Once guilt is established, the question is of determining the nature and the severity of punishment. In case the guilt is established with some scope for doubt, it should also reflect in the type of punishment and its severity. Every manager who has taken disciplinary actions knows how complicated even simple looking situations can be in reality. Therefore, this statement by Cāṇakya is to be remembered by every manager every time he thinks of enforcing rules through punishment to the rule breakers. In Ch 1 itself – *sūtras* 7, 8 and 9 – the manager has first been asked to equip himself with the right kind of worldly wisdom by learning from a mentor. One major use of this capability is in enforcing rules through the right kind of, and right severity of punishment. More on this comes later.

Enforcement of rules and laws have to be done wisely because undue harshness – as perceived by others (not by the giver or the taker of the punishment) – causes the manager to be hated by all as already told in *sūtra* 2 of this chapter. How does right enforcement of rules help to manage wealth distribution – as stated in *sūtra* 3? This is explained next.

## 12 दण्डे प्रणीयते वृत्तिः ।

*daṇḍe pra-nīyate vṛttiḥ*

Employment is sustained through enforcement (of rules).

This word *vṛtti* is again a multifaceted word which conveys 'a means of livelihood'. Retiring is '*ni-vṛtti*'. Inclination to behave in a certain way is '*pravṛtti*' because vritti also means 'nature of behaviour'. We should therefore, take both these meaning into account for interpreting this *sūtra*. *Vṛtti* also stands for the monetary and other payments offered to the job holders for doing their job as expected.

A systematic organisation of work of different kinds in any organisation is certainly based on basic rules of work, work distribution, and of behaviour at work. We talk of job elements, job description and of roles of jobholders. All these and also the payment the jobholders receive are described under the same word *vṛtti*. A major advice given to the manager in Pachatantra is "Never commit (or let happen) a '*vṛtti-bhanga*' i.e. any delayed or incomplete or less than deserved payment for a job'. If this happens, "employees capable at their job, even when they are from good families, will leave the employer."

The emphasis on a good system of rules (laws) – i.e. *daṇḍa-nīti*, and on the right type of enforcement i.e. *daṇḍa* has been justified by Cāṇakya in both negative and positive manner in this chapter. Use of *daṇda-nīti* also refers to the use of military administration and to the use of 'the science of politics', depending upon the context in which 'enforcement' is to be done.

**_Sūtra_ Summary: Enforcement**

Harsh words are worse than burns, one who gives harsh punishment becomes hate worthy by all. Non-friends are controlled through administration of justice/science of politics. People are protected through law enforcement. Control manages wealth. Without control, no set of ministers. The prohibited things are not done when enforcement exists. In law and politics, lies one's own protection. When self is protected, all gets protected. Growth and destruction are dependent on oneself.

Justice is administered through worldly wisdom. Employment is sustained through enforcement of laws.

CHAPTER 9

# ॥ अर्थः ॥

# Resources

1 वृत्तिमूलं अर्थलाभः ।

*vṛtti-mūlaṁ artha-lābhaḥ*

Obtaining money is based on employment.

Gainful employment is the only way to manage to earn money and/or to acquire other resources on a continuous and sustainable basis for every member of the society. Having stated that 'employment' of all types needed for the sustenance of any human society is possible only through the rule of law, Cāṇakya expands on the idea of earning and using resources.

The other implication of this *sūtra* is also important. No money can be gained through means other than employment. If such money is gained (e.g. through theft or through inheritance or through a lottery or through discovering a hidden treasure of some one else etc.) neither the money nor the resource generated from it will last long enough. For sustainable wealth generation for all individuals in a society, employment of useful kind for which payment will be willingly given is indeed a pre-requisite.

2 अर्थमूलौ धर्मकामौ ।

*artha-mūlau dharma-kāmau*

Ethical behaviour and fulfilment of desires are based on money.

The observation that ethical behaviour in society is dependant on fulfilling the minimum needs of all in terms of resources was made right in the beginning by (1.2) by stating "Ethics is based on resources". Here, we find the same statement repeated in the context of an individual who is earning money through employment.

An individual (person) – like any one of us – does not earn money to be able to behave ethically or to be able to follow all the different duties that inherently come to him according to all the different roles a person plays in the society. Each individual plays multifarious roles in any society: a man is a citizen, a son, a husband, a father, a brother, a friend, an employee, an employer, etc. Similarly, a woman also plays many different roles. All roles have associated duties of ethical, moral and legal kind. A person can fulfil all these duties – his/her *dharma* – only when adequate resources are earned by the person.

This aspect of earning money has to be brought out specifically because most 'religious' teachings emphasise that 'goodness' in this life and in after-life (assuming and asserting that it exists) is incompatible with going after money-earning. Becoming rich or striving to earn more resources has been looked down upon as incompatible with striving for eternal peace after death, *nirvāṇa* or *mokṣa* or whatever else the after-life is called by different religions. Earning money i.e. working for acquiring resources is a need, is a desirable task for an individual in any society that wants to sustain itself in a civilised manner.

And not just the fulfilment of duties, but also the satisfaction of desires is based on resources being available. In the Aryan culture, from time immemorial (estimates vary between 7000 BC to 4000

BC for the period in which the vedic hymns were composed) the four main achievement goals set for every human being are: *dharma, artha, kāma,* and *mokṣa,* in that order respectively and respectfully! First come the duties (ethical, moral and legal), then acquiring resources or money (through 'good; ethically permitted means), then the fulfilment of desires (including sexual, apart from just the procreational needs), and then release from the attachment to worldly affairs. Cāṇakya draws attention to the fact that neither *dharma* nor *kāma* are really possible without the possession of adequate resources. As pointed out in *Gīta, kāma* or desires are themselves a form of godliness when these are fulfilled without crossing the limits of ethics. (धर्माविरुद्धो भूतेषु कामः अस्मि भरतर्षभ।)

## 3 अर्थमूलं कार्यम् ।

*artha-mūlaṁ kāryaṁ*

Work is based in resources.

Any kind of work to be done must have resources for it to be successfully accomplished or completed. This statement or observation appears too obvious to be included as a *sūtra.* But does every single work require money or resources? It is necessary to distinguish between the words *karma* and *kārya* here. *Karma* denotes action, while *kārya* means a piece of work, a task or a job to be undertaken, pursued and completed. Actions may or may not require resources or money, but work usually would.

Some manuscripts of Cāṇakya *sūtra* have an extra word सर्वं – *sarvaṁ* – before *kāryaṁ* in this *sūtra.* It is preferable not to have this adjective which makes no exceptions possible. Especially in view of the next *sūtra* on why work is based on resources.

4 यत् अल्पप्रयत्नात् कार्यसिद्धिः भवति ।

*Yad alpa-praytnāt kārya-siddhiḥ bhavati*

Thence little effort leads to work accomplishment.

Availability of resources makes it easier to accomplish any work or job or task. This also means that a lot of efforts can possibly help to do a piece of work even when the monetary resources do not exist or are meagre.

It is important to note that money alone is not meant under the word *artha* and that the resources need not represent only their money value. Lack of tools, for example, can make a task unduly difficult. Similarly, lack of good person-to-person networking can hinder the success or reduce the speed of getting a job done. All types of resources are covered under the word *artha*, as will be evidenced from the next *sūtra*.

5 सर्वाः च संपद् सर्वोपायेन परिग्रहेत् ।

*sarvaḥ ca saṁpad sarva-upāyena pari-grahet*

All kinds of wealth/resources should be acquired by all types of means/methods.

The verb *pari-graha* means not only to acquire but also to store over a long period for retrieval and use. The usage of '*sarvāḥ ca*' is also done to emphasise all types of resources and wealth.

The message here is loud and clear. "Go all out for acquiring and storing resources of all types by as many different ways as needed." A shamelessly explicit message to all individuals – especially to all managers – for creating wealth of resources for themselves. Since ethical behaviour as well as fulfilment of desires (without crossing ethical boundaries) is possible only with acquisition of resources, and since resources help getting things done with less efforts, go ahead and acquire resources by all means, again without crossing ethical boundaries.

## 6 अर्थतोषिणं श्रीः परित्यजति ।

*artha-toṣiṇaṁ śriḥ pari-tyajati*

Wealth leaves those who are satisfied with resources (that they possess).

In chapter 7, *sūtra* 11 states that craving for money is not a counted as a vice. By now it is clear why going after resources in any ethical manner is a desirable activity for oneself as well as for the society as a whole. Now comes even a stronger advice. "Do not feel content or satisfied with whatever resources you have acquired". But typically, it is not stated in this way; only the consequences of such complacency with available resources is stated as a law: "Wealth gets dissipated when complacency sets in." Every manager – especially the CEO – must continuously be aware of this *sūtra*. No enterprise can retain its level of resources or of profitability at whatever 'high' level has been reached. The only effect of being satisfied with the performance is a gradual deterioration in resources or profits. This *sūtra* is consistent also with the definition of management given by Cāṇakya (4.6). The third element of management consists of 'growth' of what is acquired and protected. The principle is of 'growth,' not of 'maintenance' at the given level (which is just protection). Without working for growth, even maintaining the given level of performance becomes difficult to achieve.

7 भाग्यवन्तम् अपरीक्ष्यकारिणम् श्रीः परित्यजति ।

*bhāgya-vantaṁ aparīkṣyakāriṇaṁ śrīḥ pari-tyajati*

Wealth recedes from a fortunate (one) who (undertakes/does) works without examination.

A person who possess wealth of different kinds – money, knowledge, skills etc. – is a fortunate one. This *sūtra* could simply have been framed without the first word *'bhāgyavantaṁ'* i.e. one endowed with good fortune; because any one who works without examining the different aspects of work carefully would not be able to retain wealth. But then, would such a person possess wealth at all? Yes, only if he or she gets it as an inheritance or as endowment or as an elected leader by people (It may be noted that during a thousand years before and after Cāṇakya, the systems of *grāma-sabha* – village councils – and also *gaṇa-rājya* – republic territories – were prevalent in India. Leaders in village councils as well as rulers of the republics were elected persons). Such a person needs to be careful about the fortune that he has acquired. Unless the work done by him, the duties performed by him and the new tasks to be undertaken by him are done with proper thought, the wealth will dissipate. The right kind of examination of pros and cons, and consideration of the consequences that may follow from the work whether done successfully or even unsuccessfully, needs to be done for every item of work.

How to go about such examination is stated in the next *sūtra*.

8 ज्ञानानुमानैः च परीक्षा कर्तव्या ।

*jnāna-anumānaiḥ ca parīkṣa kartavya*

Examining ought to be done through knowledge and inference.

The problem that is faced most commonly by every manager is that information available for undertaking any major work or action on any new idea is never complete. Answers to many important elements of the work to be done are either only partly available, or are probabilistic, or are simply not known. Knowledge is invariably found to be not complete enough to take a unique decision – the one and only one right decision – about the work at hand. Cāṇakya was quite aware of this through his own experience in management. Therefore, he emphasises that while knowledge is the first basis for action, inference is vitally important. The idea of acquiring the right type of knowledge needed by the manager was already conveyed in earlier *sūtras* (1.5 to 8). Now logical inference is added to knowledge.

*Tarka-śāstra* or logic was part of the learning to be acquired by every person during this period of *Guru-Śiṣya* – (teacher-disciple) tradition on the Indian subcontinent. Deductive as well as inductive logic was being taught, but the emphasis was more on the deductive logic. Perhaps due to this reason, Cāṇakya does not elaborate on terms like *jnān*, *vijnān* and *anumān* in this principle of management.

After emphasising that resources are a major requirement of work accomplishment, Cāṇakya goes on to advice managers on the principles of how to manage work successfully.

### *Sūtra* Summary: Resources

Money is earned based on employment. Both ethics and desires are based on resources. Work is based on resources, since they lead to work accomplishment with less efforts.

All kinds of wealth should be acquired by all methods. Wealth leaves the one who is satisfied with (available) resources. Wealth recedes from the fortunate one who works without examining the job process. Examination should be done using knowledge and inference.

# CHAPTER 10 ॥ कार्यव्याप्तिः ॥ Working

1 उपायपूर्वं न दुष्करं स्यात् ।

*upāyapūrvaṁ na duṣkaraṁ syāt*

Attended with (right) means (any work), does not become difficult to do.

The word *upāyah* denotes a remedy or a means to accomplish anything; it also stands for efforts, exertion. Politically, as a means of success against enemy, it refers to the four ways of *sāma, dāma, daṇda* and *bheda* i.e. persuasion, payment, threat and separation. In the present work context, it stands for an appropriate means or an effective method of doing the work successfully.

This statement about using the right means is in a non-negative form: using the right means or method a work does not become difficult to accomplish. It is not said that work accomplishment becomes easier with the use of right means. Knowing the complexities of real life that result in unexpected disturbances in any work planned by the manager, this statement says that without right means, difficulties will arise in implementation in desired manner: i.e. with less efforts, time and cost etc.

This *sūtra*, taken with the earlier one on strategy (3.1 – All new work must be *mantra* based), tells the manager how carefully any work programme must be pre-planned giving due attention to the means to be employed for carrying out the work.

Does this statement on 'means' appear to be too obvious? Experienced management consultants will be able to cite numerous instances where poor conceptualisation about the means has resulted in failures or in inordinate delays.

Cāṇakya elaborates on strategy in the next 2 *sūtras.*

2 अनुपायपूर्वं कार्यं कृतमपि नश्यति ।

*an-upāya-pūrvaṁ kāryaṁ kṛtaṁ api naśyati*

Work (done) without (proper) means gets destroyed (later) though accomplished.

This is a strong statement. A manager may feel happy and proud after a task gets successfully accomplished. However, if the proper means or effective methods were not to have been followed, the result would not be sustained for any worthwhile period of time. The temporary advantage from work would dissipate away soon, and the work system would go back to the same state as in the past or could get even worse. Cāṇakya warns the manager that he should not become complacent about any success at work wherein he is not sure about the way in which the desired result-success-has come about.

3 कार्यार्थिनाम् उपायः एव सहायः ।

*kārya-arthināṁ upāyaḥ eva sahāyaḥ*

For those who want to accomplish work, right means alone is the help.

After stating that work accomplishment becomes less difficult when the right means are used, and that success achieved without such use would not last, it is time to emphasise that the only real help for managers in accomplishing the work is the right means. One reason why Cāṇakya speaks about the means and the method of doing the work so emphatically could be that the means are included in the five-fold project planning process of *mantra* only for "the beginning" *(ārambha-upāyaḥ)*. The conduct of the work itself would require the use of the suitable means.

The use of the plural form for the doer of work is significant here. It indicates generalisation of the statement as well as points towards team work. Several persons would normally be involved in accomplishing a task and all should be aware of (and trained in) using the pre-planned means or method.

4 कार्यं पुरुषकारेण लक्ष्यं संपद्यते ।

*kāryaṁ puruṣa-kāreṇa lakṣyaṁ saṁpadyate*

Work goal is reached through manly efforts.

The word used here is not just effort, but *puruṣ-kāraḥ* i.e. manly efforts or prowess (as opposed to relying on fate or luck). This can be considered to have a specific meaning which encompasses the two elements in control of the 'doer', namely 'means' and 'efforts' as explained in the context of *vinaya* – humility and discipline (1.5-6). These two elements have to be appropriately managed to suit the task at hand. This kind of doing work is *puruṣa-kāraḥ*. The goal set for any task undertaken by a manager – any doer – by himself or through others, is achieved through sustained efforts of the right kind and by using appropriate means.

That the planned strategy by itself does not accomplish any task, and right kind of efforts by capable people using appropriate means are needed for it is too obvious to state. Perhaps, Cāṇakya wanted to emphasise on this aspect because the motivation for sustained efforts is not easy to find. Many a tasks fail to achieve their intended results because not enough is done. One concludes too soon that either the expected result is beyond one's ability or that one is not lucky enough. That's what the next *sūtra* talks about.

5 पुरुषकारम् अनुवर्तते दैवम् ।

*puruṣa-kāraṁ anu-vartate daivaṁ*

Luck follows - chance becomes favourable - (when) manly efforts (are put in).

We have seen earlier in Ch 1 that a 'doer' ought not to feel vainly proud when the desired result occurs (i.e when he is successful), nor ought he be dejected and feel miserable when the opposite of the desired result happens to take place (i.e when he is unsuccessful). This is because the fifth basic element of all 'actions' is 'chance'. After reading this *sūtra* we realise that the words in the previous *sūtra* were carefully chosen. The right type of efforts lead towards accomplishment of the goal – they do not invariably result in achievement of the goal. The element of chance always exists, because the result of even simple actions or work are dependent on too many factors external to the situation, and beyond the control of the doer. Keeping this in mind, any person who undertakes any work or action needs to choose the efforts and the means in such a way as to maximise the chances of success. This is precisely the message from this *sūtra*: luck can only follow the right efforts by right means put in by the right doer.

When the desired result does not occur while attempting for it, the *sūtras* 4 and 5 convey a good message. Re-examine all four elements other than chance underlying accomplishment of any work or action: the basis, the doer, the means and the efforts. Experience of previous failure and observation/interpretation of unexpected direct or indirect results are good teachers for the manager who takes the trouble to stop and to introspect. In a surprisingly high number of situations where success seemed to have eluded the doer, the culprit is found to be the 'basis' itself! Many a managers would be able to recall work situations where the premise on which actions were based turned out to be wrong or inappropriate or non-existent!

## 6 दैवं विना अतिप्रयत्नं करोति यत् तद् विफलम् ।

*daivaṁ vinā ati-prayatnaṁ karoti yat tad viphalaṁ*

The excessive effort that is made without luck is fruitless.

If all the efforts done using the right means do not give the desired result, and re-examination of the first four elements brings out that nothing was really inappropriate, then luck is certainly not with the doer. The 'doer' should then cease to work on this particular task, because lots of efforts etc. cannot and will not lead to success. It is better to wait for 'something' in the work environment to change .... which it usually does as time passes – before re-starting efforts. Or, if one can afford to do so, simply give up on the end result as 'impossible'.

We can quote a *'subhaṣit'* from Bhartuhari here to confirm this philosophy of looking at work and its successful accomplishment. उद्योगिनं पुरुषसिंहम् उपैति लक्ष्मी । दैवम् हि दैवम इति कापुरुषा वदन्ति ॥ दैवम निहत्य कुरु पौरुषं आत्मशक्त्या । यत्ने कृते यदि न सिध्यति कः अत्र दोषः । *udyoginaṁ puruṣa-siṁhaṁ upaiti lakṣmi, daivaṁ hi daivaṁ iti kāpuruṣa vadanti. daivaṁ nihatya kuru pauruṣaṁ ātma-śaktyā, yatne kṛte yadi na siddhyati kaḥ atra doṣaḥ*. "Wealth goes to the industrious person. Only the non-performers leave everything to fate. Leave aside fate and put in all your efforts. If, inspite of putting in efforts, success is not achieved, where is the blame?" In other words, neither the doer should blame himself nor should his boss blame him for failure.

In real life, the individual who fails gets dejected because he starts feeling that he is not competent enough to ensure success. He considers himself in a poor light and becomes despondent about failures etc. Similarly, the boss feels that the person who made the failed attempt is not competent enough etc. though the boss himself had found it not possible to detect any flaw in the first four elements of that work which failed! It is in this context that this philosophy of looking at work helps the manager to function without undue stress from work, and also to remain enthusiastic for future work in spite of failures.

Thus, we see that the thought process underlying the *sūtras* 4, 5 and 6 in this chapter serves a very useful purpose of defining an excellent ethos for managerial work. Capable managers, who have carefully nurtured humility of the right kind, will not only put in a large amount of well-directed efforts the first time, but will also review their scheme of work if success eludes them that first time. If no element were to have been at fault, they would not re-launch efforts. They will work enthusiastically in spite of non-success, without getting dejected by failures. They 'know' that 'success' is not under the 'control' of the 'doer'.

7 पूर्वं निश्चित्य पश्चात् कार्यं आरभेत् ।

*pūrvaṁ niścitya paścāt kāryaṁ ārabhet*

Work ought to be started after deciding earlier (planning).

That any new piece of work to be undertaken should preferably take the form of a project planned by the manager has already been stated earlier (3.1). Spend effort, time and energy on planning the work: do not rush into actions without pre-planning.

What kind of 'decisions' can be taken 'earlier'? That is, before even undertaking the work? The pre-planning involves generating several alternative ways – action plans - to reach the desired goal, of considering the consequences of each alternative in terms of impact on events and on persons; of inferring about the possible reactions and actions of those impacted by the planned action either directly or indirectly, and then thinking through the possible actions the manager can take to counteract the undesirable consequences. It is a veritable game of chess in real life – the more the number of moves the manager can foresee and plan for, the more likely he is to achieve success.

Work pressures, urgency of taking some action, pressure from bosses or from rival enterprises are the kind of external forces that make a manager take up action or new work in haste, without the due process of planning and strategising. There also exist internal forces such as an unduly heightened sense of capability, a disdain for slowness in action and a sheer neglect of the processes at work because of arrogance arising out of the power position occupied by the manager. It is necessary to guard against such forces which continually act on managers. Cāṇakya, aware of such situations, has felt the need to stress the planning process by devoting a *sūtra* to it.

## 8 कार्यान्तरे दीर्घसूत्रता न कर्तव्या ।

*kārya-antare dīrgha-sūtratā na kartavyā*

No procrastination ought to be done between works.

Here is the advice for avoiding 'Paralysis by Analysis'. The word *antara* stands for the interval before starting a work as well as intervals between successive sets of actions in a work process or between successive work items. Immediately after stressing the need for pre-planning, comes this advice on not taking too much time for the business of planning or thinking about the future sets of actions. 'Undue delays in taking decisions about the next action' is a very commonly observed managerial failure. Granted that 'inaction' or 'action at a suitably later time' is sometimes a better alternative than 'a quick action', even this is a 'decision' that must be taken without undue delay. 'No action' in such a case should not result out of a non-decision or because of the manager's inability to decide upon an effective action plan. The decision making process has to be quick enough and definitive enough to manage the situation properly.

Where should a manager draw a line between 'due consideration' and 'undue delay'? Obviously, all such terms are relative, and will change with several factors connected with the work item. A good way to learn is to introspect on past experiences of success and failures with special reference to 'timing'. Another is to obtain feedback from seniors, colleagues and juniors on what they perceive. Ultimately, of course, the 'decision' will rest with the manager himself on 'how much' time to spend on planning and on the decision making process!

9 असमाहितस्य वृत्तिः न विद्यते ।

*a-samāhitasya vṛttiḥ na vidyate*

For one who is not calm (and composed), employment does not exist.

Cāṇakya takes us back to the facts that the resources are generated by employment, and the work gets accomplished through resources. Now, if the worker – the doer – the manager – does not understand the framework of thinking behind putting in the right type of efforts to reduce the chances of non-success, he would always remain tense, not calm and composed with a balanced outlook. He would not manage the work well. The consequences of such non-management or mismanagement would be the eventual loss of his employment. However, the words used are not for such a person who has lost his job. A person devoid of this work ethos can find himself in any of the following situations:

a) To begin with, he will not put in efforts to obtain a gainful employment
b) If pushed in a position to have to work for a living, he would do it without applying his mind, and make a mess of the job more often than doing the job well
c) At work, he will get jubilant and complacent on 'success' and dejected and despondent on failure. His boss and colleagues will find it difficult to deal with such a moody person.
d) After a failure or two, he will give up all enthusiasm for work and will only 'do what is told' – another recipe for continual failure.
e) In all these situations, he will experience considerable mental stress at work, since no one – including himself – will be

satisfied with the state of affairs. These tensions would lead to mental and/or psychosomatic disorders.

These and possibly other consequences would ultimately mean that this person is not fit for employment. No position would suit him. It may be noted that *vṛttiḥ* also means profession, cause of activity, and respectful treatment. For the imbalanced person, these too will be missing.

## 10 न चलचित्तस्य कार्याव्याप्तिः ।

*na cala-cittasya kārya-āvyāptiḥ*

No work completion for one with vacillating mind.

Many a managers embark upon a piece of work after some pre-thought, but get doubts or second thoughts about whether the action already initiated upon is the right one. Such a manager then changes the decision, not just once, but perhaps several times. The work is then in a mess. It does not get either fully done or done well in time.

If the manager finds himself in a situation where he just cannot decide upon which action plan to choose from amongst the several available to him (generated by him and others), the consequences are equally disastrous. He may end up doing too little, too late. The work will not get accomplished.

Another interpretation of the word *āvyāpti* is the work management in terms of finishing a number of work pieces within a reasonable time i.e. the time management. A manager with an indecisive, vacillating mind will pick up an item from the 'in-tray', ponder over it, and keep it for a fuller consideration at a 'later time'. Most often, between 'this time' and 'later time', no fresh input of information is likely to occur, even if attempted by this manager. In such cases one could as well take a decision 'now' rather than 'later'. Such postponement of decision making invariably means increasing the amount of time spent on the same items of work many fold. Such wrong time management leads to much fewer items of work getting done in any given time interval. The work-load overwhelms the vacillating and procrastinating manager, and many work items remain pending – unaccomplished.

## 11 हस्तागतावमानात् कार्यव्यतिक्रमः भवति ।

*hasta-āgata-ava-mānāt kārya-vyati-kramaḥ bhavati*

Ignoring that which has come into (your) hands causes work to be not done properly.

*Vyatikrama* means deviating, non-performance, omission and reversal, among the several meanings that this word has. These indicate the nature of disturbances to proper work, that can arise by ignoring or belittling what you already have.

Every manager desires to have more information, more help by way of assistance from employees, larger budget for expenditure etc. for the work allotted to him or taken up by him. Each CEO is familiar with the fact that the sum-total of 'demands' or 'requirements' given by all departmental/functional heads put together usually exceeds the available resources by a factor of 2 at least! This is a typical situation which occurs essentially because managers tend to take for granted that available resources are inadequate. Most often, this is not their deliberate stance: it so happens that they fail to address the situation with the assumption that the allotted task(s) must be completed with 'what they have in their hands'. If a detailed planning exercise (3.1 & 10.7) shows that some crucial resource is unavailable, or if some additional resource can speed up the work substantially, or can improve the quality of work significantly, then and only then, would a manager be justified in asking for 'more' of any resource.

The wording is not *'hasta-gata'* (already available in hands), but *'hasta-āgata'* (what has come into one's hands). This signifies that the manager should not only consider the resources he already has, but also those which can be acquired with the available resources with ease. Such resources are almost like those which are already in hand, provided the manager applies his mind to the situation and strives for accomplishing the given work without seeking extra resources. Asking for more resources is the easiest way out for avoiding responsibility for work completion: any manager can ask for more, and most do it most of the times. Hence this *sūtra*.

### *Sūtra* Summary: Working

Use of right means makes for fewer difficulties. Even the work accomplished without appropriate means does not last. For work achievers, right means alone is helpful. Work goal is reached through manly efforts/prowess. Luck follows such efforts. One's excessive efforts without luck become fruitless. Start work after planning earlier. Do not procrastinate while at work.

One who is not composed has no employment. One with vacillating mind cannot accomplish work. Ignoring that which has come into hands, causes non-performance at work.

# CHAPTER 11 ॥ कार्यम् ॥ Work

1 दोषवर्जितानि कार्याणि दुर्लभानि ।

*doṣa-varjitāni kāryāṇi dur-labhāni*

(Items of) work without any fault are seldom found.

Here comes a profound statement of fact from the first management guru of the world: no managerial task or action can be expected to be free from all faults. Some or the other 'fault' – a negative aspect, an adverse impact etc. – is associated with almost every single action or piece of work proposed to be undertaken by a manager. However, this *sūtra* does not categorically say that all work pieces must have some fault or the other. Cāṇakya prefers to err on the safer side, perhaps for the fear of being contradicted by thinking students, who may then dilute this advice too much. Since it is very rare to find any action or job which is totally free of faults of some kind or other, the manager must not waste his time or defer an action or a decision till such a time that a faultless alternative is found.

One of the modern advice is 'let the best not be the enemy of the good'. This *sūtra* has an identical implication. A manager in search of the perfect, fault-free work, would not take a good enough action when it needs to be taken. Thereby, the work may not just get delayed, but may also fail in reaching its proposed or planned end result.

A manager must understand this principle clearly and take an effective action which will maximise the chances of success and minimise the chances of undesired direct or indirect consequences. It is not surprising that the 'Case Method' developed by the Harvard Business School in late 1950s emphasises the fact that there exists no unique, right decision in any real life situation. An experienced manager seeks to develop the most effective – the least defective – action plans. He is aware that almost every managerial action gives rise to unexpected and often unforeseeable consequences, which again need to be dealt with suitably for the work plan to succeed.

## 2 दुरनुबन्धम् कार्यम् न आरभेत् ।

*dur-anubandhaṁ kāryaṁ na ārabhet*

A task with bad consequences ought not be started.

Having stated that faultless jobs are difficult to come across, Cāṇakya immediately speaks of one category of jobs which are just not worth undertaking. This category is defined by him as of consisting of those tasks for which the manager sees that the end result will be uncertain owing to major un-surmountable difficulties coming in the way; where he cannot see a proper course of action. Of the 18 meanings of *anu-bandha*, 5 seem to be applicable here: Coomencement, continuous flow, motive or cause of action, repeated application and (good or bad) result/ consequence. If there exists any known difficulty at the commencement of the work itself, or in managing the assignment in a continuous manner, it is better not to start the work. The manager should first try to remove the known or most likely impediments and then start the work. If the motive behind starting the works is itself 'bad' or if the results after the completion of the work are likely to be bad, it is better not to start the work. The word 'bad' as a meaning for *dur* is to be used not only in the ethical sense, but also in the sense of undesirability in terms of the objectives of management (gains, protection and growth of wealth). It is unlikely that the sense of 'difficult for repeated application' is implied in this *sūtra*, for all work assignments. Only those kinds of assignments where successful completion once does not mean much unless repeated applications are made can be subjected to this advice on 'not starting' the work.

The *sūtra* does not say 'do not start difficult (*duṣkaram*) work'! The skill of any competent manager is to undertake and to successfully complete difficult tasks: his total training is towards this goal.

## 3 कालविद् कार्यम् साधयेत् ।

*kāla-vid kāryaṁ sādhayet*

The knower of time should accomplish work.

The manager who understands the two aspects of time-timeliness and time management – would be in a much better position to successfully complete the work. Having started a work for which the course of action is properly planned irrespective of success or failure, managing the 'timing' element becomes critical to success. All managers learn from their experience in dealing with other persons that a good idea expressed at the 'wrong' time fails to get accepted by the boss (or colleagues or even juniors). The same idea or suggestion, framed or expressed in the same way, 'clicks' when the timing is right.

Cāṇakya does not elaborate on how to impart this skill for judging timeliness, like he does not talk about any other skill development. The need for a skill is stated. The method of developing the skill to the extent that it got internalised by the disciples/students would have been the mentorship and the role model provided by the Guru. It is a pity that 'discussion notes' on these *sūtras* were not developed by a Guru like Cāṇakya to train other 'teachers' to teach these *sūtras*. Or, it could as well be that such notes existed but were not preserved for the posterity by those who ensured survival and propagation of these *sūtras* through rote.

The other aspect is time management. How much time to spend on each item of work, how to delegate to reduce self involvement, how to prioritise work items, how not to 'waste' time etc. will be covered under the part of work time management. Cāṇakya covers several of such ideas on work as he proceeds with his teachings.

4 कालातिक्रमात् कालः एव कार्यं पिबति ।

*kāla-atikramāt kālaḥ eva kāryaṁ pibāti*

With passing away of time, the time itself swallows up the work.

If the manager does not take timely action, or if too much time is allowed to pass before any action is decided upon, this inaction over a time period causes the work to perish. Another intepretation of the word *ati-krama* is neglect: neglecting time as an important factor in ensuring successful work accomplishment leads to failure. It is as if the time itself has eaten up (drunk) the job at hand!

5 क्षणं प्रति कालविक्षेपम् न कुर्यात् सर्वकृत्येषु ।

*kṣaṇaṁ prati kāla-vikṣepaṁ na kuryāt sarva-kṛtyeṣu*

1. Let seconds not be scattered away in all the actions that ought to be taken.
2. An opportune moment in taking all dutibound actions should not be (lost owing to) confusion about timing.

Given the different meanings of the words and the context of preceding and succeeding *sūtras*, both the translations given above appear to be appropriate. The use of the word *kṛtya* in place of *kārya* in this *sūtra* is significant: not work or job assignment, but actions seem to be involved here.

Passing of time or 'neglecting time' is a broad, general statement, as given in the previous *sūtra*. Here, attention is drawn to the fact that small, negligible looking time intervals tend to accumulate because of indecision or procrastination or even owing to a feeling such as 'awaiting some other event' etc. Seconds accumulate and the manager awakens to discover to his dismay that the right action has been delayed by several days. Therefore, this advice on not neglecting 'seconds' (incidentally, *kṣaṇa* equals 'four fifth of a second' as a measure of time.)

Quite often, 'timeliness' is critical. The right action taken at the right moment makes a tremendous difference to the probability of success of a work assignment. Such moments cannot be pre-planned. The manager has to be alert to the situation to be able to say the right things in a manner which appeals to the person – decision maker – with whom he is pleading for getting something done. Many of us are aware that we have either missed such a good opportunity or bungled it up by not being able to use the right words backed by appropriate body language. The second meaning of this *sūtra* is meant for this kind of situation.

6 देशकालविभागौ ज्ञात्वा कार्यम् आरभेत् ।

*deśa-kāla-vibhāgau jnātvā kāryaṁ ārabhet*

Work should be started after knowing the two aspects: place and time.

For any job to succeed, the answers to the question of where and when to start have crucial importance. This "where' refers to two different aspects of 'place'. The cultural background or the socio-political background of the people is one aspect. It has to be understood before undertaking any managerial action. Whether such an action is to encourage desirable behaviour or to discourage undesirable behaviour, its success would certainly depend on how it fits with the existing culture. Even work items which are not expected to influence the behavioural pattern of the people of a particular place may invite unexpected adverse emotions, leading to failure. The other aspect of 'place' is the immediate physical surrounding where the work is to take place. Some consideration needs to be given about 'the place' in which the beginning of an important work is to be planned. Whether the initiation of a new work idea should be done in a close door meeting with one or two selected persons, or whether it should be breached during an official lunch or thrown across while playing golf is a decision every manager has to take.

The 'when' part of the question refers again to two aspects of timing – one in the general sense of socio-economic circumstance under which the work is to take place. We do know of several examples where pieces of work based on essentially good ideas or concepts turn out to be non-fructuious because these are 'before their time' in a society. Similarly, examples are seen of 'being too late' to implement a kind of work, which could have succeeded in the atmosphere which existed say 10-15 years ago. This kind of timeliness of the work is an important consideration for a manager who wants to undertake a major task. The other aspect of 'when' is short-term: which time of the day, after which event takes place in the next few days; under which frame of mind of the person on whom the start and the conduct of the work depends etc.

The advice by Cāṇakya to every manager is: "Be aware of the external factors of time and place, study them carefully, understand their implications to the work you plan to start. Only after you consider all these and feel that these are 'ripe' in a general sense, and know that you can choose them in a particular sense, should you start work". This is a good practical advice for enhancing the chances of success for the work to be started. This is one major part of pre-planning as advised in 10.8

## 7 दैवहीनम् कार्यम् सुसाधम् अपि दुःसाधं भवति ।

*daiva-hīnaṁ kāryaṁ susādhaṁ api duḥ-sādhaṁ bhavati*

A luckless task, even when easy to accomplish, becomes difficult to conduct.

Time and again, we see this kind of a reference to fate, destiny or chance. After all, many managerial experiences do show that what one considered to be simple, easy to manage jobs do not get successfully done because of several unexpected difficulties which are beyond the control of the 'doer'. At such times, the conclusion 'chance' or 'fate is not favourable now' is to be preferred to a conclusion in the vein "I am no good" or "so and so is against me". In other words, a self-dejecting or another person-baiting type of 'person oriented' conclusion is to be avoided. This does not mean that the manager should not analyse carefully the causes of difficulties: only the unexplainable difficulties in work are to be attributed to non-favourable chance. This way of looking at non-success also opens up several possibilities of managing the same work successfully under favourable time and place elements, again to be chosen after careful analysis before re-starting the work.

8 नीतिज्ञः देशकालौ परीक्षेत ।

*nīti-jnaḥ deśa-kālau parīkṣeta*

The (politically) wise ought to examine the place and time (aspects of work).

The wise manager has started a piece of work with appropriate pre-planning and after examining the aspects of time and place for the start of the work. Even so, several unexpected difficulties occur to prevent successful completion of the work. Then it is not enough to conclude that chance is not in favour: a re-examination of the time and place aspects becomes desirable. In fact, Cāṇakya directs the manager to undertake such a review of an ongoing work. The conclusion after such a review can be of two kinds: work towards eliminating obstacles coming in the way of accomplishment by suitable actions, or to stop the work, abandon it for now.

Another meaning of the word *nītijnaḥ* is 'one versed in politics': this meaning too is applicable in management of work in any organisation. A re-examination of time and place for a work is indeed a political skill.

9 परीक्ष्यकारिणी श्रीः चिरं तिष्ठति ।

*parīkṣya-kāriṇi śrīḥ ciraṁ tiṣṭhati*

Wealth stays for long with the one who (so) examines, and works.

Why all this advice to the managers about how to start and to accomplish work? The objective of all managerial work is wealth generation. Cāṇakya does not let his management students lose sight of this main goal of management of any enterprise. Gaining what is not with you, maintaining it and then making it grow, through deployment of people (4.8) constitute management. This is a continuous process where every work item has to be carefully considered for implementation, and implemented well through an equally continuous examination of the factors which are affecting its success. The wealth remains for long only with those managers who keep examining their work progress in such a careful manner.

### *Sūtra* Summary: Work

Fault free work is rare. A task with bad consequences should not be started. The knower of (right) time, accomplishes work. With passage of time, the work vanishes. In all actions, do not neglect seconds. Start any work after knowing the implications of place and time. A luckless task, though easy, becomes difficult. So the wise should continuously examine the place and time. Wealth stays for long with one who so examines.

# CHAPTER 12 ॥ कार्यार्थिः ॥ Work Manager

1 दुःसाधम् अपि सुसाधं करोति उपायज्ञः ।

*duḥ-sādhaṁ api su-sādhaṁ karoti upāya-jnaḥ*

The knower of right means makes even difficult (jobs) easy to accomplish.

This *sūtra* is a sequel to the earlier one (10.1) stating that the right means help by way of reducing difficulties in the way of work accomplishment. Therefore, a well trained manager, who understands the importance of means, uses them to manage the work more easily than in their absence. Those without such an understanding about the importance and need for the right means, would mostly launch new work assignments and then discover on the way during implementation that disturbances and blockages occur unexpectedly.

The other meanings of the word *upaya*, namely remedy, and strategies, efforts etc. are also meant in this *sūtra*.

An important part of the overall strategy is selection and placement of persons to implement the strategy. Without the right 'people support', no strategy can get correctly implemented, nor the means properly used. Therefore the next *sūtra* is on this point.

2 यः यस्मिन् कार्ये कुशलः तं तस्मिन् एव योजयेत् ।

*Yaḥ yasmin kārye kuśalaḥ taṁ tasmin eva yojayet*

One who is skilled (proficient) in a particular job should be deployed for doing the same job.

That a specific statement of this kind comes under principles of management is not at all surprising: what is startling is that this statement was made 300 years B.C. It is even more interesting to know that almost identical statements are found in Pancataṅtra and Hitopadeśa, and Cāṇakya himself states that he has carefully analysed the treatises on government-*arthaśāstra*-of his several predecessors. So, we can infer that this type of thinking was a known part of the principles of management since about 1000 BC to 1000 AD in India. This *sūtra* has several interesting implications, apart from not making a mess of the job by putting 'a square peg in a round hole'. Firstly there would be no place for solely hereditary positions at any level in the hierarchy at workplace. A non-proficient heir should not be put in position. Just as this important principle was not followed by many a rulers in India during the better documented period of Indian history (after about 800 AD) so was it not followed by many an industrial houses during the early period of industrialisation in all countries, including in India. Even Cāṇakya would not have implied by this *sūtra* that the next king be chosen based on capacity to rule! With the exception of the Top Position, this rule would be considered applicable everywhere. The good kings then and the good Indian industrialists of the recent times have found a good compromise by not necessarily handing over the reigns to the eldest son: the sons are tested through giving increasingly difficult assignments, and the best of the lot called the *karta* (doer) – is chosen to lead the enterprise.

The second implication of this *sūtra* is that there is no place for nepotism when running an enterprise. Earlier on (2.10), Cāṇakya had advised not to consult someone just because he happens to be a friend. Even 'the wife's brother' – the most delicate of 'near' relations to tackle – should not be given position which he would not deserve by merit.

The third implication is that factors such as the caste in which a person happens to born, his mother tongue, his religion, his state of residence etc. should not be considered relevant for employment (The caste or the *varṇa* concepts were quite strong at the time of Cāṇakya. At the same time, the rigidity of invariant association of craft or work occupancy with caste had not entered the Indian society. *Arthaśāstra* mentions 'If Brahmins are in the business of selling liquor, they should be considered as Vaishyas). Given Cāṇakya's times, this was a strong statement: it continues to be strong today in India where such prejudices are still at work. Even in the technologically and economically advanced societies of North America and Europe, prejudices of colour of the skin, religion, and economic class persist even after a 500 years of efforts to eliminate them, and continue to play some role in job placements and promotions. The world is witnessing an increasingly greater acceptance of the principle of equal opportunity to all, and all nation states have adopted market economy which ensures that only the efficient enterprises survive. This rule stated by Cāṇakya for excellence in management, which was too often not followed, has been adhered to strictly by excellent managements in all countries in all times.

The third implication is that corruption – accepting a bribe for giving appointment in a position – was not permitted. Not so much because it is unethical but because it can – and usually does

– hurt performance at the job. This is not a far fetched interpretation: Cāṇakya has talked specifically about '*upadhā-śuddhaṁ*' (tested for corruptibility and found pure) in the context of appointing ministers (2.11). This policy at top levels has to percolate down to the lowest level to ensure good performance at the job.

Obviously, the modern methods of testing a person for inherent skills – aptitudes – even before giving training in suitable skills and imparting relevant knowledge – were not discovered at that time. We surmise that most of the training would have been 'on the job' and the selection of 'who is right for the job' was done from amongst several aspirants. Cāṇakya does describe the attributes of a 'trainable' person in Arthaśāstra, thus helping the selection process.

## 3 अज्ञानिना कृतम् अपि न बहु मन्तव्यम् ।

*a-jnāninā kṛtaṁ api na bahu mantavyaṁ*

When performed (successfully) by a non-knowledgeable (and non-skilled) person should not be considered worthwhile.

This *sūtra,* as the next to the previous one, comes as a surprise. One would have expected that this place be the right one to talk about the adverse consequences of giving a job to a non-skilled person. The mess created by an incapable person is rather obvious to everybody, including the junior most in any hierarchy. These juniors and colleagues may not have any inkling about what precisely the mistake was or where an action or a decision was inappropriate; nor would they be capable of thinking through the right or the more effective action. But they certainly see the adverse consequences and talk about them and their implications.

This presumably is the reason why Cāṇakya does not talk about this negative aspect of a wrong placement.

Cāṇakya is more concerned about situations where the top management mistakenly comes to a conclusion about the capability of a person whose given assignment (first in any specific area) happens to be neatly carried out. Any 'success' – i.e. getting the expected result from an action – can be sometimes fortuitous. Circumstances being favourable, the expected result comes through, without any real application of mind and/or use of skills by the 'doer' of that action. At such times, top management would tend to conclude that this particular person is 'capable' unless they look carefully at all the factors at work. If they do discover that this person did not apply his mind and does not really possess the requisite knowledge and the skill, then they better not give any importance to the fact that the particular piece of work was done well.

In the 'personnel appraisal systems' of the present era, it would be good to be able to analyse in this manner the major aspects of performance and of achievements of individuals. Good managements do allow for factors such as 'difficulty of assigned work' and 'favourable circumstances' while judging 'failures' and 'success' of individual managers in the assignment done by them over the period (usually one year) under review.

4 यादृच्छिकत्वात् कृमिः अपि रूपान्तराणि करोति ।

*yadṛcchikatvāt kṛmiḥ api rūpa-antarāṇi karoti*

Accidentally (irrespective of own will) even a worm makes transformations.

A metaphor is used to illustrate the 'process' under consideration and to emphasise the point. Do we praise a pupa for its ability to turn into a butterfly? What credit does the poor thing deserve? Whether it wills it or not, it is destined to – it is programmed internally to – get converted into a butterfly. The same way, in favourable circumstances, certain tasks become successful neither because of the doer of the task, nor because of the doers efforts. These were destined to succeed, since the specific set of favourable circumstances, outside the control of or outside the influence of the doer were favourable for the expected to take place.

We note that Cāṇakya uses similes and metaphors very carefully. These could have been given almost for every second *sūtra*, but he does not do it for three reasons. First, the lesser the number of *sūtra*, the better it is for memorising and for impact. Secondly, only a few ideas which are either difficult to perceive or are difficult to accept need to be so emphasised. Thirdly, excessive use of similes or metaphors will dilute the sense of emphasis where it is needed most. This particular *sūtra* about 'not giving credit for success' under specific circumstances is one such 'difficult' observation.

## 5 सिद्धस्य इव कार्यस्य प्रकाशनम् कर्तव्यम् ।

*siddhasya iva kāryasya prakāśanaṁ kartavyaṁ*

Only the completed (successfully) work should be made known (announced).

After giving advice on assigning the right person for a job to ensure good implementation of a planned strategy, Cāṇakya turns to other aspects of managing work assignments.

A manager should not publicise or talk about any planned work or any work in progress: he should talk about it only after it is successfully carried out. The *sūtra* typically mentions only the second part of this statement. Brevity and a positive attitude are the reasons.

This advice is to take care of the political aspect of any work situation. Every organisation has to have politics at work, either positive and work supportive, or negative and disturbing work flow. Individuals not involved in the assignment have benevolent or malevolent intentions. The benevolent are OK, but the malevolent can be of two kinds. One kind wants to usurp the credit for good ideas etc. and may steal a march over the current work group. The other kind is destructive: they would sabotage the work through direct or indirect means. There exists, unfortunately, also a third category of outsiders who do not intend to be either for or against success of the specific assignment about which they come to know the details. These often naive and sincere persons commit unintentionally errors of omission or commission which result in the work getting sabotaged.

So, why invite such possible intentional or unintentional political disturbances while working on any assignment? Better talk about the assignment openly only after it is completed as planned. That also, if the manager who does the work finds it desirable. That is why the verbal form used is *kartavyam* not *kuryāt,* which would have been a directive to do so always.

6 ज्ञानवताम् अपि दैवमानुषदोषात् कार्याणि दुष्यन्ति ।

*jnāna-vataṁ api daiva-mānuṣa-doṣāt kāryaṇi duṣyanti*

Even for the knowledgeable (and skilled), work assignments get spoiled owing to adverse fate and/or due to human faults.

Work being done even by capable persons can get spoiled due to chance or due to human interferences of the kind described in the previous *sūtra*. Therefore, a manager should better not talk openly about his assignment, or of its success, or of the benefits that would accrue on its completion. Even when chance is the operative reason for non-completion of the work or for the failure of the assignment, the position of the manager who has talked openly about his assignment becomes laughable, at least somewhat awkward.

This *sūtra* helps a manager to realise that a failure does not necessarily mean that he is incapable or non-knowledgeable. He need not feel personally dejected when he knows that he has used the right knowledge and skill while performing the task, but success has eluded him. In such cases of failures, he should analyse the possible other reasons for failure: namely, actions of other persons or chance. In fact, this type of analysis should not wait till the work is over. The verb in this *sūtra* is in the present tense – which is also the form used as a present continuous tense in Saṇskṛt. A manager working on an assignment starts getting a feel on how it is proceedings. If he starts experiencing difficulties which would possibly lead to failure, he should look at 'what' is causing such difficulties. When he, and his team-mates on the assignment, cannot discover any 'human factor' causing these troubles or difficulties, he should conclude that it is only fate or chance as the cause for disturbances of unknown and/or known but non-controllable factors on the result of the actions.

7 दैवदोषम् शान्तिकर्मणा प्रतिषेधयेत् ।

*daiva-dosham shānti karmaṇa prati-ṣedhayet*

Adverse fate should be propitiated through peace-ritual.

Those who believe in supernatural power of some kind or the other, to which human beings can appeal for help (and, hopefully, receive it too,) do undertake rituals to propitiate such a power. In the Indian system of thought since over 7000 years BC, this belief in supernatural power existed. It took many forms of rituals and worships, but the ritual used to appeal to one or more such (powers or) gods of specific functions before starting any major work or assignment of even occupying a new house etc. was termed *śānti-karma*. This *karma* or a specified ritual would invite the appropriate god to look after the conduct of the work, to ensure that its conduct would not be beset with any undue difficulties (to shoo away evil influences), and to ensure that ultimate success is achieved. Cāṇakya, in the same tradition, recommends this *śānti* ritual.

We note that such traditions have a very strong hold on the minds of people in general, and Indians in particular, even in the 21st century. All major projects in public and private sector, all building constructions, almost all house-warming are started after some such ritual by Hindus, Jains, Buddhists, Sikhs and Parsis. Since most of the Christians and Muslims in India are converts from Hinduism, most of them seem to also follow this tradition in their own way. Being connected with the concept of a Godhead which helps when worshipped, it is difficult to prove either that such a ritual is useful or that it is meaningless or non-useful. Even if properly designed scientific experiments were to prove to the contrary, 'faith' in such rituals is difficult to shake or to eradicate. (The best example of this phenomenon is the faith in Astrology.)

However, it is good to note that the verb form used is *prati-ṣedh* – i.e. to work in opposite direction/to drive off. The idea behind conducting such a ritual is to reduce the probability of failure or to reduce the difficulty in conduct of an assignment. The next *sūtra*, where human behaviour is dealt with, uses a verb form meaning 'to remove' or 'to eliminate'.

## 8 मानुषीं कार्यविपत्तीम् कौशलेन विनिवारयेत् ।

*mānuṣīm kārya-vipattīṁ kauśalena vi-nivāryet*

Manmade difficulties in the work should be skilfully eliminated.

Though the word used is *doṣaḥ* (a fault) in the sixth *sūtra* which speaks of the two types of disturbances in work and the same word is continued in the context of fate or chance (which was translated as 'adverse fate'), it has been dropped when actually dealing with the human factors. These are not faults that occur on their own, these are deliberate difficulties started or introduced by others – human beings – who, for various reasons, do not want the work to succeed; or by those who inadvertently cause difficulties in the execution of the work.

Such difficulties should be skilfully removed is the advice. This skill would be of various kinds: consulting them before or during the assignment, involving opinion leaders in decision making,use of tact, persuasion, incentives etc. If necessary, use of appropriate force or pressure, including threats etc. of the right kind. Using an appropriate skill to specifically remove a particular type of human difficulty may have been illustrated through anecdotes by Cāṇakya during the course of his teaching the students. If so, those anecdotal illustrations have been 'lost' to posterity.

9 कार्यविपत्तौ दोषान् वर्णयन्ति बालिशाः ।

*kārya-vipattau doṣān varṇayanti bāliśaḥ*

The immature (persons) narrate mistakes/faults when difficulties (arise) in work.

Every CEO is familiar with this type of human behaviour: the reasons why or the excuses for any work assignment not getting completed successfully and/or in time. Those who have been assigned work, and find it difficult to manage it well, tend to find faults with the situation or with other people etc. This 'facility' to complain is not available to the top man, who has to say 'The buck stops here'. This is the attitude recommended by Cāṇakya by saying that those who describe faults etc. are really childish, they are not willing to take the responsibility on themselves to ensure that the given assignment is conducted properly on their own. A manager should neither behave childishly like this nor permit others to whom he has given work assignments to behave in this manner. He would need to show by example, and offer coaching and guidance, to develop the right attitude among his juniors. Sometimes, he may also have to set example for his colleagues.

*Bāliśaḥ* also means the foolish, the ignorant and also careless - those who do not take up the work seriously enough.

## 10 कार्यार्थिना दाक्षिण्यं न कर्तव्यम् ।

*kārya-arthina dākṣinyaṁ na kartavyaṁ*

Work achiever ought not to show kindness (softness).

Many a managers are taken out of the race to reach the top position because they are somewhat 'soft' or a little too considerate of other person's feelings when it comes to taking an unpleasant step. Several occasions arise where such kindness, considered otherwise 'good' in personal behaviour, comes in the way of accomplishing the work efficiently and successfully. Cāṇakya advises that if a manager wants to be successful in managing assignments well, he better not fall prey to such 'kind' considerations.

Giving corrective feedback to juniors is a necessary part of developing them into efficient work achievers. This feedback, being based on a negative aspect of the work being done, is unpleasant to give. Soft managers avoid giving such feedback or procrastrinate. In either case, not only does the work in hand suffer, but the junior (sometimes even a colleague) fails to learn the efficient way of work accomplishment, thus affecting his future capability.

When someone has dilly-dallied at work, taken it casually or given it in an unauthorised way to some one else to do etc. he needs to be quickly pulled up. Again an unpleasant task, which needs to be managed frankly and fairly. When the junior has failed because of carelessness or because of not enough efforts or not sufficient application or mind, this needs to be pointed out promptly.

Sheer indiscipline of different kinds takes place at every work place. "This is not my job", "I will not do it", "That other fellow has less work, why catch me for everything", "I already have too much work" are the refrains that one hears continually in any organisation. These appear to be fair statements and sometimes really are. But experience shows that such perceptions are often not valid when tested factually: and the manager has to be a 'boss' enough to say it candidly.

This list of managerial actions where a kind of ruthlessness is needed in tackling people at work can be expanded indefinitely. At the other end of this spectrum of actions is removal of the person from the job. Tough managers take such tough decisions in their stride, while still being humane and tactful. It sounds surprising indeed that all tough but fair decisions receive approval of most employees, including those directly affected by the decision. In one sense, it is not all that surprising, because every employee understands within himself the need for such actions in the interest of the continued survival of the business organisation, whether in manufacturing or in service sectors, in which he works.

## 11 क्षीरार्थी वत्सः मातुः उधः प्रतिहन्ति ।

*kṣīra-arthī vatsaḥ mātuḥ-ūdhaḥ prati-hanti.*

A calf wanting milk hits against mother's teats.

Pat comes another of Cāṇakya's metaphor. Is 'hurting' some one justified in getting 'work done'?

Those goody-goody human relationists or those spiritually endowed souls who consider all others just like own self may have even theoretical objection to such a statement on how a manager should behave! Even good intentioned capable managers sometime wonder whether the kind of tough step they are about to take against someone – i.e. a step to modify an inappropriate behaviour of a junior – is 'proper' or 'justifiable to one's own conscience'. Such persons need to be conveyed that the right spirit behind those tough actions which should not be avoided by an effective manager.

This metaphor, indeed, serves this purpose very neatly. Why does the calf need milk? For his survival and growth. He does not wonder whether the action of sucking would hurt the mother cow. In fact, after initial feed, he literally has to hit at the teats to get his full. The cow gets hit alright, but this hitting does not hurt, even when repeated at every feed. The mother cow, too, is relieved at the end of the process. What would happen if the calf decides to be kind and not hurt the mother even a little? Both will suffer. That is exactly what would happen if the manager acts 'soft' at times when 'tough' action is needed: he himself, the junior concerned and the organisation would all suffer adverse consequences from such soft options. Experienced managers know that 'softness' of this kind has a way of spreading a little too fast in an organisation — downwards and across the hierarchy. It is necessary to avoid acting 'kindly' in every single situation that invites avoidance owing to its 'unpleasantness' in the overall interest of the organisation.

## 12 अप्रयत्नात् कार्यविपत्तिः भवति ।

*a-prayatnāt kārya-vipattiḥ bhavati*

Lack of effort turns into difficulties in work.

After starting any specific task, if continuous and sufficient efforts are not exerted to make things happen in a way favourable to work accomplishment, the result is not just stagnation, but an increase in difficulties in the work on hand. (The prefix *a* stands for none or less in the word *a-prayatna*.)

In other words, no work or job remains in the same state if efforts are ceased for some time or inadequate efforts are put in. The work situation deteriorates in such a way that success becomes increasingly difficult to achieve. Having said earlier that a politically suave manager – *nītijna* – should consider the time factor (11.6, 11.8) carefully, this type of further advice becomes necessary. If actions are stopped mid-way because of any reason, this kind of passage of time through non-action is not good. Most often, such pause in efforts would not be desirable.

## 13 न दैवप्रमाणानां कार्यसिद्धिः ।

*na daiva-pramāṇānāṁ kārya-siddhiḥ*

No work accomplishment for those who consider that fate alone decides.

The word *daiva* – fate, destiny or chance – keeps on popping up in these principles of management. As we have seen in the very beginning (1.5) while commenting on development of *vinaya* or humility, *daiva* or chance is the fifth inevitable element of any work or action to take place. Once the manager has attempted to overcome adverse fate by the peace-ritual (13.7), he may then take it easy and say "It now depends upon luck. If it is favourable, my work will get done the way I want it. If not, what can I do?" This attitude of considering luck or fate as supreme is to be avoided. Such managers, states Cāṇakya, will not be successful at work. They will not get the desired result. Here, the statement is not probabilistic like "The chances of success would reduce". This is a definitive statement that if a manager put trust in fate, he will surely not succeed.

There exists a rather delicate balance between active efforts using appropriate means by the doer, and abandoning futile efforts after noting that chances of success are too small. Where to draw the line of demarcation, where exactly to stop further efforts on a difficult task is almost always an inituitive decision, a decision based on the gut feeling of the manager. Managerial experience helps to sharpen such gut feelings, but no such decision is known to be the right one when it is being taken. Even future results/ events do not necessarily tell the manager whether the decision for stopping efforts was right. The only exception is of the cases where the abandoned task is taken up later at the right time and place, and thereafter happens to succeed.

## 14 कार्यबहुत्वे बहुफलम् आयतिकम् कुर्यात् ।

*kārya-bahutve bahu-phalaṁ āyatikaṁ kuryāt*

When the number of tasks are many, priority should be given to (that work) which is most fruitful.

Having advised on time management earlier (11.3 to 5), Cāṇakya now talks about prioritising the assignments. The basic objective of management being wealth generation, preservation and growth, priority should also be always given to work items which give more advantages. This is equivalent to an 'In-basket' training exercise devised for the modern manager. This training exercise helps the manger to differentiate items as with high, medium, and low priorities, based on several criteria. The most important amongst them being the 'benefit to cost' ratio. Any action or type of work which gives a high gains with relatively low input costs or time or efforts etc. should naturally be given priority.

Another reason for including this type of an obvious looking statement as a specific *sūtra* would be well understood by most managers: the unfortunate tendency to give priority to the 'urgent' rather than to the 'important'. Every manager is flooded with too many items to be 'cleared' immediately, within the day, at the most. These could as well be 'C' items, in the ABC categorisation of importance. Most such 'C' items are best delegated to the lower levels to ensure that only the A items, and few of the B items reach the top level. In fact, this method of not allowing C items to reach one's desk needs to be followed by managers at all levels.

Many an item which are vital to the survival and growth do not form a part of the in-tray of a manager. These crucial aspects - usually of strategy planning like modernisation of machinery or systems etc. – are indeed those which give 'many fruits'. But these are not felt as a part of daily work pressure by the manager. It is important to give priority to such work items.

## 15 स्वयम् एव अवस्कन्नं कार्यम् निरीक्षेत् ।

> *swayam eva avaskannaṁ kāryaṁ nirīkṣeta*
>
> Failed/Improperly done jobs must be examined only personally.

The fourth element of Cāṇakya's definition of management is 'through deployment of persons'. Most of the work that manager does is the work he gets done from others, mostly his juniors and also his colleagues. As stated in the preceding *sūtra* on prioritisation of work, delegation of work of low importance to lower levels is a worthwhile proposition. But even after guiding

A & B priority tasks through suitable decisions and actions, situations do arise where the work does not get done satisfactorily. When the employees are well trained and properly guided, such 'unsatisfactory' results would be rare: say, less than 1 in 100. Cāṇakya's advice is clear: "Do not accept at face value the reasons given by those who have executed the work for its non-successful completion or its non-completion etc. Go and examine the situation by yourself." Even when the employees entrusted with the task are sincere and competent, an experienced senior often finds some deficiency in work or in the thinking of the juniors, which could probably have lead to the observed failure. When he, too, cannot find such removable deficiencies, his critical examination is worthwhile to gain confidence in the capability of the juniors. Then, together with the juniors or by himself, he can attempt to achieve the same end result by a different route altogether.

This *sūtra* also makes it clear that blaming the juniors for non-success is not the right attitude for a manager. After all, if under the guidance of a manager, the work does not succeed, then who is responsible and accountable? Only the manager: if he complains about work difficulties, he is branded 'immature' by Cāṇakya.

If a manager has to examine failed (or not properly done) work items too often, should he stop doing so? Not quite: then he must realise that either he has chosen the wrong persons to delegate the work or the guidance given by him was not appropriate to the task. Introspection can help him to improve on both counts and then to reduce the proportion of failed items.

Another equally important implication of this *sūtra* is that the manager should not normally be involved in details of all work which he gets done. Once delegated he should not 'keep observing' all the time. This type of over-supervision is bad in several ways: it not only wastes the precious time of the manager but also demoralises the persons carrying out the work. They tend to pass on the responsibility for work accomplishment upwards, do not learn to find their own solutions for even minor difficulties they come across etc. Training others to accomplish tasks successfully is good for all concerned. And when one is sure that the delegated job will be done well, there is no need to supervise all the time. The manager does not have to know precisely how a job was well done; he wants results and when he gets them, all he should do is to give a 'pat on the shoulder' to express appreciation and to encourage the employee to undertake even more responsible work in future.

### *Sūtra* Summary: Work Manager

The knower of right means makes difficult jobs easy. Place a person in job for which he has skills. Accomplishment (of work) by an unskilled person is not to be given importance. Even a worm undergoes transformations!

Publicise only completed work. Even for the knowledgeable, work gets spoiled through adverse fate and human faults. Adverse fate should be propitiated through peace-ritual. Human difficulties in work should be skilfully removed. Those who complain of difficulties in work are childish. A work achiever ought not show kindness, like a calf desiring milk hits at mother's udders. Less efforts make for obstacles in work. For those who depend on fate, there is no work accomplishment.

Give priority to the most fruitful work when faced with many assignments. Examine by yourself any failed job.

# CHAPTER 13 ॥ कार्यसिद्धिः ॥ Work Accomplishment

1 कार्यबाह्यः न पोषयति आश्रितान् ।

*kārya-bāhyaḥ na poṣayati āśritān*

One who keeps outside of work does not feed (nurture) dependants.

The words used are 'feed dependants', since the age of Cāṇakya was of a feudal system of governance. It would be more appropriate in the present context to transliterate these words as 'nurture the employees', without stretching the meanings of the *Saṅskṛt* words *poṣayati* and *āśritān*.

The term *kārya-bāhya* appears to be an interesting jargon in managerial behaviour. The reference here is presumably not to a manager who has no work for a certain time period, nor to a manager who happens to not do the allocated work etc. This term would specifically refer to that kind of manager who avoids assuming the responsibilities appropriate to his position in the organisational structure and consequently, does not play the role he is expected to play. He effectively keeps himself away from that work which truly belongs to his role as a manager. Obviously, he does not say 'No, this is not my work' or 'I will not do this work'; he only behaves in such a way that it becomes apparent to all that this manager is not 'in his work' – he is like an outsider or like an observer.

What happens when a manager is of this type or when he behaves like this? Cāṇakya does not refer to the effects of this on the manager's work: he prefers to draw our attention to another, more important aspect, which is not so obvious. Such a manager will not bother to assess whether the staff strength available to him is adequate for the job, and if not, recruit few more employees. He will not evaluate the capabilities of his staff nor help them to grow in their capabilities for the work in hand or for future work needs. In fact, he would have no involvement in such nurturing of his employees. This consequences is far more troublesome to the organisation in the long run, than the short-term consequences of a job or two not getting done or getting done only partly.

It is worthwhile to note that not all tasks belonging to this '*kārya-bāhya*' managers role will get disturbed since his juniors would manage most jobs well on their own. An outside observer or even the manager's boss may not notice much going wrong with the ongoing work items. Cāṇakya's advice, therefore, is to judge a manager's performance on this criterion of "Does he nurture his employees?" Only a good manager fully involved in his work will feel the need for grooming his staff in technical and inter-personal skills needed to accomplish work successfully and smoothly. A manager who keeps away from such grooming is likely to be '*kārya-bāhya*': present physically in his position but not really 'in position'.

2 यः कार्यम् न पश्यति सः अन्धः ।

*yaḥ kāryaṁ na paśyati saḥ andhaḥ*

One who does not see work is blind.

One major reason for a manager to be 'outside of work' is that he does not 'see' any work that he must do or should do in his role. He takes his position for granted and feels that others below him will anyway execute the work to be done. He is either detached from his role or is so carefree that he does not even think of what role he needs to play to be an effective contributor to the organisational goals. Such a person is termed as 'blind' by Cāṇakya. The very position of a 'manager' is created to get things done without having to tell what, when and how to do the required work. A manager is expected to generate work. If a person needs to be told 'what' to do, then such a person is an assistant or a helper or a worker, he is not a manager. The basic role of a manager is to think through and to do whatever is necessary to fulfil the responsibility he has been assigned. To decide upon the question "what to do", is primarily his responsibility. When a manager is a little perplexed about what to do, he may use the *sūtra* 8 of chapter 3, look at policies to think of what (and how) needs to be done. He may use others – juniors, colleagues and even seniors – as sounding board(s) to test out his ideas on 'what'. He should also be alert to spot good ideas generated by others - especially the juniors - who should be encouraged to think of new ideas and to express them freely. But the primary responsibility of generating ideas is his. On the question of 'when' too, the prime responsibility is his. The 'how' part is split into two aspects: 'through whom' and 'in what manner'. Here, the manager would do well to take participative decisions.

These two *sūtras* (13.1,2) are good tools for managers to undertake a periodic self-assessment. "How often have I been *kārya-bāhya* and/or *kārya-andha* in the past 3 months?" "What were the adverse consequences of my lapses in these aspects?" "Why did they happen and how, therefore, can I manage to avoid them in future?"

These are also good tools for senior management to judge the performance of managers. A manager found prone to such lapses needs to be counselled and improved. If such improvement does not take place, then better remove 'the blind' and give that position to a person who can 'see' what work he ought to do.

3 प्रत्यक्षपरोक्षानुमानैः कार्याणि परीक्षेत ।

*pratyakṣa-parokṣa-anumānaiḥ kāryāṇi parīkṣeta*

Works (jobs/assignments) should be examined through self-observations, others' observations and (logical) inferences.

The idea that the time and place must be first examined while undertaking any work assignment or even when conducting it was covered earlier (11.6, 8). These are sort of external parameters for any work. Now three internal parameters are being mentioned. First come the observations or the considerations or even the feelings of the manager himself. Second are of those others who are involved or associated in doing the work, or of those who are willing to share their experiences of similar earlier work without necessarily being connected with this specific assignment. The third parameter for 'examination' of the work assignment consists of drawing logical inferences from what has been observed or felt directly or indirectly. Application of this type of logic would often bring out inconsistencies in observations, missing steps in courses planned for action, vagueness in work formulation, or even such things as low probabilities for the occurrence of expected events or results of actions etc. This kind of three fold examination would naturally lead to improvements in planning and conducting the work assignment, leading thereby to an increased probability of successful completion of the assignment.

## 4 अपरीक्ष्यकारिणं श्रीः परित्यजति ।

*a-parīkṣya-kāriṇaṁ śrīḥ pari-tyajati*

Wealth deserts the one who works without examination.

Back again to the central theme of wealth generation, maintenance and growth. The inevitable consequences of not doing every single work with a thorough examination is that the wealth dissipates away. That a manager who is not thorough in his work will not be able to generate wealth is obvious. But even protecting what you happen to have earned from past good work or inherited from predecessors would not be possible, if the manager does not 'see' what work he needs to do, and/or does such work in a slip-shod way without applying his mind to it.

Why should the manager examine every assignment in this three-fold way? Cāṇakya does not guarantee success for the work or even mention that the particular work will not succeed. He warns the manager of a long-term consequences of getting into the habit of doing assignments in a routine manner, without applying his mind to it fully. The so-called adverse effects of one or two assignments so carried out may not be visible, leading to slowness or to complacence. A manager must be particular that such a situation does not occur any time if he wants to protect and to grow the wealth that exists already.

## 5 परीक्ष्य तार्या विपत्तिः ।

*parīkṣya tāryā vipattiḥ*

Difficulties ought to be resolved through examining.

The method for examining an assignment before starting and also in an on-going manner, as well as the consequence of not keeping the prescribed three fold vigil on assignments were stated in the previous 2 *sūtras*. This *sūtra* states the purpose of such examination: resolving difficulties that come in any work assignment. The use of the verb *tār* is to be noted: it denotes 'swimming through' the difficulties. The verb used does not indicate 'removal' or 'elimination' of obstacles that come in the way of completing the work. As every manager is aware, only a few of the different kinds of obstacles in work can be truly eliminated. In most cases, the manager is constrained to find ways of managing the work – reaching the planned gaols – even when the expected or unexpected difficulties continue to exist. That is whey the English word used in translation is 'resolved' rather than 'solved' or 'removed'.

The objective of continuously examining each work assignment through personal observation and available means; through getting a feedback from others involved as well as not involved in the work, and through logical inference is to resolve difficulties that keep coming in the smooth conduct of work assignment. The classification of difficulties into two causes – fate and manmade – has already been mentioned earlier (12.6, 7, 8). Cāṇakya advises the manager not to let down his vigil after starting even a well-planned work (3.1), started after carefully considering the elements of time and place.

6 स्वशक्तिम् ज्ञात्वा कार्यम् आरभेत् ।

*sva-śaktiṁ jnātva kāryaṁ ārabhet*

One should start work knowing own capability.

This is a rather obvious looking statement: who would want to take up work beyond his own capability? Obviously, every manager works within his area of skill and competence: a civil engineer by training would not venture to manufacture machines; or a lawyer would not want to treat an ill person. The reference to capability here is naturally meant for work assignments within the skills and knowledge the manager possesses. But then, whoever really knows precisely what his capability is? In fact, there really exists no way to find out 'how much I can accomplish' for any person, any manager. The only way a good manager discovers his own capacity is to stretch himself to achieve high goals, and in case he does not succeed in spite of all 'examination' and efforts, then to conclude that either fate is against him or he has attempted something beyond his capabilities.

A top ranking management Guru that Cāṇakya was, he knew these facts about the 'strength' or 'capability' of a manager. That is why he placed this *sūtra* after talking about all other aspects of starting and managing work.

This *sūtra* could possibly have come in the last but one chapter (11.6), along with the *sūtra* on starting work after considering time and place. But it does not: and we should acknowledge the importance of its location in the sequence of Cāṇakya's aphorisms on management.

## 7 स्वजनं तर्पयित्वा यः शेषभोजी सः अमृतभोजी ।

*sva-janaṁ tarpayitvā yaḥ śeṣa-bhoji saḥ amṛta-bhoji*

One who enjoys out of the remainder after satisfying own people enjoys ever-endingly.

As soon as work is accomplished – and each managerial task aims at generating wealth/resources – the question of distribution of money, perquisites, status, position etc. come up and need to be effectively dealt with. That is how this *sūtra* follows after the work difficulties are resolved. In his holistic way of looking at management, Cāṇakya is seen to shift from the general to the specific, from managing others to managing oneself, from acting as an employer to acting as an employee, and from time management ideas to "human resource' kind of staff ideas with an ease that can come only through long managerial experience coupled with an extraordinary insight on processes of management.

The verb *tarpa* is difficult to translate into English. In the Indian culture the reverence given (offered) to any guest – even uninvited and unexpected guests – is very high. It is considered the bounden duty of a family to not only welcome him into own household, but also to satisfy his wishes. A little inconvenience to oneself or to other member(s) of the family, or even some sacrifice of self-interest, is not supposed to matter at all – it is just done. This kind of satisfying the needs or desires is denoted by the verb '*tarpa*'. The verb form used is not '*toṣayitva*', which would have denoted the simpler concept of satisfaction in the normal sense.

The wording used is very specific about what the manager should claim from the wealth resulting out of the work done; from that portion which is left over after satisfying those who are 'your own' people, some of whom have directly helped you in the specific task that has been accomplished. The process is not the other way sound – namely, take what you want because you are the boss who managed the work – and then distribute the remainder amongst your men! Again, this is a prescription, not an order or even a directive by Cāṇakya. He knew the strength of avarice on one hand and the futility of giving moral advice on the other hand, especially to a person in position of power. So, he – in his typical way – brings home to the manager the consequence of his recommended method; and that, too, by giving such a manager an epithet reserved for the gods - the enjoyers of nectar of immortality. The word *amṛt*, which literally means nectar, is in fact a combined word from *a* and *mṛt* , meaning 'no-death' – i.e. immortality. In the context of management, which is always for wealth generation, the implication of this *sūtra* is clear: the process of wealth generation and the enjoyment of the fruits of the generated wealth becomes a sustainable (long-lasting) process when the wealth is first equitably distributed amongst the employees (and also partly saved for future contingencies) and then taken by the top management for satisfying their own desires (We talk about the 'desires' and not the 'needs' at this level of wealth availability, which is far above the 'needs', even when defined comfortably!).

## 8 सम्यग् अनुष्ठानात् आयमुखानि वर्धन्ते ।

*samyag anu-ṣṭhānat āya-mukhāni vardhante*

When all (this) is followed, the sources of income increase.

The 'sources of income' have been specified in Arthaśāstra (68-14) as seven different ways a ruler of kingdom or a government of a state can generate its income needed for governance. These need not be relevant to a business enterprise and so will not be enumerated and discussed here. The concept, however, is worth examining by itself.

The basic idea is to continue the earn more, generate even more wealth. Therefore, to constrain oneself to only the presently available means of income is not proper. Different business ideas for generating income need to be continually thought of and tried out on an appropriate small scale. Those amongst the new avenues of income which show a greater promise for growth should be pursued and the remaining phased out.

This kind of gradual increase in the number of sources of income – different business units of a large enterprise – is made and sustained through the generalised advice given till now on how to start new work and how to manage it appropriately.

However, the form of this *sūtra* is surprising: it almost states a law in the present tense that 'following good practices at work causes the sources of income to increase' It is not clear why Cāṇakya does not say that 'in order to be able to increase the sources of income, conduct all work properly'.

### *Sūtra* Summary: Work Accomplishment

One un-involved in work does not nurture employees. One who does not see work, is blind. Jobs should be examined by observation by self and others, and also through inferences. One who works without examination loses wealth. Difficulties are worth resolving through examination.

One should start work after knowing own strength. One who enjoys after satisfying own persons, enjoys for long. When all is adhered to, the sources of income increase.

CHAPTER 14

# ॥ लोकः ॥
# Human Relations

1 न अस्ति भीरोः कार्यचिन्ता ।

*na asti bhīroḥ kārya-cintā*

The timid does not care about work.

A manager must keep on thinking about how best to manage the present work, and to plan for the future work. He is all the while concerned about work since it is only through successful accomplishment of the work that he contributes to the goal of wealth generation. But a manager who is unsure of himself, not clear in his thinking, is unable to take right decisions at the right time. As a result, he avoids taking decision, he becomes timid... afraid of taking up any responsible work etc. Such timidity simply means that he is not concerned enough, does not care enough about the work that he should be doing as demanded by his role of a manager.

Another implication of this *sūtra* is that a manager who ceases to care for his work, even temporarily, is exhibiting timidity: an attitude no manager would like to be associated with his name. 'Do not be timid at work' is the message.

2 स्वामिनः शीलं ज्ञात्वा कार्यार्थी कार्यम् साधयेत् ।

*swāminaḥ shīlaṁ jnātvā kāryārthī kāryaṁ sādhayet*

Understanding the character of the boss, the work-manager should accomplish his work.

Most managers, of necessity, have a boss, a superior who has larger powers of decision over larger functional areas of the enterprise. Therefore, every manager has to not only get the boss helping him in his work, but also has to ensure that the boss does not come in the way of success of the work for any reason whatsoever. And the bosses are – unfortunately as well as fortunately – in a position to help or to hinder the work through intentional or unintentional acts of commission or omission. 'Managing the boss' is thus a known need of almost every manager. Cāṇakya shows his awareness of this fact by stating this *sūtra* after all others about work accomplishment: even if all other 'things' are examined properly before and after starting work, success can be managed only if the work is carried out in a manner that is acceptable to the boss.

However, every boss has his own convictions about work methods, about people management and about resource availability etc. As a human being, he has his own peculiarities which are to be understood and used, rather than critically analysed and judged as 'right or wrong'. Some bosses would delegate completely, after explaining in detail; others will give brief instructions, expect the junior to do his own thinking and to come back for further clarification, if any. Some may wish to publicly give credit to the junior managers and others, while some would be unhappy if the credit is not given to them by juniors in an explicit manner. Some feel very proud when asked for guidance, others look upon the junior with disdain if he seeks advice. Some would ask 'Tell me what more you want to accomplish the (high) goal' and give it quickly if convinced of its reasonability. Others would enjoy their status by first refusing, and then graciously accepting, every single fair and justifiable demand on resources. Some bosses love to talk a lot, some use words very sparingly. Some are moody, get angry quickly, but do not keep that anger as a grievance against the junior for long. Others, cool and suave, may possibly be vindictive. This kind of listing can be increased ad infinitum and ad nauseum! – since all of us are humans with our own weaknesses and strengths. As an experienced management Guru, Cāṇakya here tells the young trainee manager about the need for 'managing the boss' for successful work accomplishment.

3 धेनोः शीलज्ञः हि क्षीरं भूङ्क्ते ।

*dhenoḥ śīlajnaḥ hi kṣīraṁ bhūṅkte*

Only the one who understands the character of the cow savours the milk.

Cāṇakya wants to emphasise this need for 'managing the boss by giving this metaphor immediately. But more importantly, he wants to demonstrate that the need as well as the lead role here is that of the manager, and not of his boss. This relationship with the boss is to be managed not by the boss but by the manager himself.

After all, this working with the boss – not for the boss, but for the organisation – is a process, not a one-time affair. It is necessary for this relationship to be a 'win-win' relationship for the manager and his boss. If it becomes a 'loose-win' or 'win-loose' relationship, it will cease to be a continuous process. This process can be either 'a vicious circle' of continually deteriorating relationship; or 'a virtuous circle' of continually improving relationship.

Both these aspects are brought out well by this metaphor on cow's milk: The one who desires to get milk – success at work – has to handle the cow – the boss – well, after understanding its (his) nature – to ensure that the process is continuous.

## 4 क्षुद्रे गुह्यप्रकाशनम् आत्मवान् न कुर्यात् ।

*kṣudre guhya-prakāśanaṁ ātma-vān na kuryāt*

Giving out confidential information to the lowly (persons) should not be done by the self-possessed (manager).

Having spoken about a number of 'Dos' about how to manage work, Cāṇakya now turns to the 'Don'ts'. His first don't about managing work assignments successfully is not to indulge in the comfortable pass-time of talking about the work with those who are available to listen and are willing to admire, but are placed low in hierarchy or in positions which have nothing to do with the work in hand. A week or an insecure or a boastful manager tends to divulge confidential details about important assignments to such idle persons, essentially to show off his own importance. This is not the kind of behaviour which a wise manager with good self-control – one who has managed *indriya-jaya,* i.e. conquered the organs – should ever indulge in. The adverse impact of such indiscriminate disclosure of confidential aspects of work is many fold: vital information reaching the 'wrong' persons would almost always lead to sabotage of the work. "Why create difficulties? Better control yourself."

The other aspect of confidentiality concerns the personal aspects of the managers life, including his personal thoughts about work situation. These, too, should not be talked about with other persons, unless needed for a work objective.

## 5 आश्रितैः अपि अवमन्यते मृदुस्वभावः ।

*āśritaiḥ api ava-manyate mṛdu-svabhāvaḥ*

Even the juniors disobey the mild-natured.

The verb *ava-man* has several meanings: to belittle, to disregard, to condemn, to think linghly of. All these apply here well! The word *āśrit* means 'dependants', but has been deliberately translated as employees in the present context. *Mṛdu* means soft, tender, delicate, mild, weak, feable, slow, among others. All these meanings, too, apply well here.

The statement tells the manager the unavoidable consequence of being – and/or being perceived as – a weak or soft person: namely, his orders or instructions or advice will neither be heeded nor carried out. This kind of a mild manager will often fail to accomplish work successfully. His juniors will hold him in low esteem.

The implied message to the trainee manager is: "Do not be soft, be strict when it comes to getting work done the way it needs to be done."

## 6 तीक्ष्णदण्डः सर्वैः उद्वेजनीयः भवति ।

*tīkṣṇa-daṇḍaḥ sarvaiḥ udvejanīyaḥ bhavati*

The harsh enforcer becomes worthy of disgust from all.

But being strict does not mean that the punishment to be given for not following the instructions or for breaking the rules of behaviour laid down by the organisation for all employees should be harsh. Here, the 'punishment' is not meant to be of the judicial kind, but of the kind that a manager will give to his juniors to ensure obeyance as well as discipline. As we know, such punishment can take several forms: from simple verbal pulling up to 'dismissal from service'. What is the consequence, according to Cāṇakya, of being habitually over strict – i.e. of always giving stronger punishment than considered appropriate? Such a manager would become 'worthy of disgust from all'. Let us consider this wording carefully. Firstly, it is not stated that all will get disgusted or feel afraid of him. Though worthy of disgust, fear, etc. some like minded may even admire him. Secondly, not only the affected person, but other juniors, too, will feel like distancing from him or will get annoyed at his stricter than necessary punishment. The 'all' also includes colleagues at the same level of hierarchy and those at the senior levels. These, too, get annoyed because this kind of 'wrong' behaviour, as perceived by most employees, results in alienation of the employees from the management, and thereafter, from the goals to the organisation. The feeling of 'we' and 'they' often begins from such behaviour from the managerial cadre. Such actions, over a long time period, lead to accumulation of annoyance, which can result into a mild hatred, which eventually can explode into the form of strong rebellion. Cāṇakya has already stated earlier (2.3) that the anger of the employees is the worst of all angers. So, let the manager be aware of this kind of consequence of setting up such wrong practice of too harsh punishments while managing people at work.

## 7 यथार्हदण्डकारी स्यात् ।

*yathā-arha-daṇḍa-kārī syāt*

Become one who punishes as deserved.

There exists a fairness in justice, there exists a fairness in punishment, and there exists also a reasonably common agreement amongst people on what constitutes such fairness. Obviously, we need to accept also the fact that this fairness is relative over time and place in the sense that it is governed to a great extent by the culture of the 'people' amongst whom this justice and punishment is to take place (Cutting off the hands of a man for rape could be considered a fair and just punishment in the 17th century India, but not in the 21st!). Most managers have had to take disciplinary actions for misdemeanours of various kinds and degrees. The moment such a decision on punishment is taken, there could be a general hue and cry about it being too much etc. We know that most of this is political noise of the right kind, which needs to be made by different affected quarters. However, whenever fairness has been exercised, transparency has been maintained and it is made clear that the punishment is for ensuring non-repition of unwanted behaviour (please refer *sūtra* 7 in Chapter 8) by the person being punished (and by others, too), even those people who are non-friends would agree that such punishment was needed in the interest of the organisation. Instances of labour unions not opposing even dismissal of their member who has committed a big misdemeanour are known.

A manager should be aware of the consequences of being too strict in giving punishment (previous *sūtra*) and, therefore, strive to ensure that the punishment to be given is appropriate to the magnitude of the misdemeanour in terms of its effect on the functioning of the organisation. Cāṇakya gives a directive here: "Be a manager who ensures that the punishment to be given is appropriate to the extent and magnitude of misbehaviour".

8 अल्पसारम् श्रुतवन्तम् अपि न बहुमन्यते लोकः ।

*alpa-sāraṁ śrutavantaṁ api na bahu-manyate lokaḥ*

People do not respect a person of low capability even if he is knowledgeable.

In the context of how a manager is perceived by others, i.e. by the employees and by the circle of their acquaintances outside the organisation, Cāṇakya has already made two observations. If seen as 'soft', the manager will be ignored; if too strict, the manager will cause ill-will. Now comes the third observation. If perceived as wanting in strength, vision, energy, heroism, courage, firmness, excellence (all these are meanings of *sāraṁ)* the manager will not be admired by people.

Capability is the ability which is used to get the desired results from every assignment taken up by or given to a manager. This capability has two constituents: knowledge and skill. Both these, in turn, have two components: technical and human. Cāṇakya is referring to the consequence of a technically knowledgeable and skilled manager who is seen not to accomplish work well. Such a manager would be seen as 'not good enough' by the employees because he falls short on abilities like vision, energy, courage etc. as mentioned above. He would not command respect and consequently, would not prove to be an effective leader of people.

## 9 अतिभारः पुरुषम् अवसादयति ।

*ati-bhāraḥ puruṣaṁ ava-sādayati*

Overload causes the manager to be exhausted/disheartened.

Quite a few 'do's' have been prescribed for the manager. Indeed, he has been advised to work enthusiastically and with energy to accomplish his work. He has been told to be alert all the time – to ensure following the ethical path, and not miss the right opportunity, to be wary of using unduly harsh words or of giving harsh punishments etc. It is time to also tell him not to be workaholic. If the workload and also the stress from his work becomes too high, it would have several consequences. The three main ones can be expressed by just one verb *ava-sad*. In its causal form it means 'to make exhausted', 'to make disheartened' and 'to make perish'. We may as well consider that the consequences of over work arise in that order: first as mental and bodily exhaustion, then a disheartening owing to perceived low accomplishment relative to effort, and thereafter the mental/physical collapse. The duodenal or intestinal ulcers, the blocked veins and heart attacks are almost invariably psycho-somatic dissorders. These affect the managerial class on a much greater scale than those in other occupations of lesser responsibilities.

The manager who has conquered his organs and also is in full control of himself, is expected to work enthusiastically but in a detached manner whereby he is aware that as a 'doer' he cannot control the 'results' of his actions. Such a manager, who has learned to manage himself, should also be aware that over work has bad consequences. Even if such a manager works 18 hours a day, say, his stress level would not increase to a deleterious level. He, being human, would possibly get temporarily exhausted or disheartened, but can spring out of the situation fast enough to remain physically unaffected. On the other hand a manager who becomes a manager, or reaches a managerial position without having learnt to manage himself first, would normally get stressed continually. Not only will his stress level for any given level of workload be higher, but also the time duration for which it lasts will be much longer. Consequently, the physiological after effects of stress would be manifest themselves sooner or later, but with a very high probability.

Typically, Cāṇakya does not advise the manager 'not to overwork'. He knew very well that, from time to time, the consciensious manager will need to put in marathon efforts as situations demand. He, therefore, only makes the manager aware of the possible consequences of over work. Knowing these adverse consequences, he should ensure that a continuous need for 'overwork' does not exist. Work must be planned and delegated suitably to right persons (recruiting new, if needed) to ensure an appropriate workload for himself. The same advice applies to work at all levels of management, and it is the duty of the top management to ensure that no manager is overworked continuously.

### *Sūtra* Summary: Human Relations

The timid does not care for work. Know the character of the boss and accomplish work. One who understands the character of a cow, enjoys milk. A manager in control of himself should not share confidences with the lowly. Even the employees belittle a soft manager, but one who gives too harsh punishment becomes hateworthy of all. Therefore, be a manager who punishes as deserved.

Employees do not respect even a knowledgeable person if he is short on strength/energy/courage.

Overwork causes a manager to be fatigued and disheartened, ultimately to get destroyed.

# CHAPTER 15 ॥ साहसम ॥ Managerial Actions

1 यःसंसदि परदोषान् शंसति सः स्वदोषं प्रख्यापयति ।

*yaḥ saṅsadi para-doṣan śaṅsati saḥ sva-doṣaṁ pra-khyāpayati*

The one who announces faults of others in an assembly, he declares/makes known his own fault.

The meetings of officials or in assemblies where many employees are present, it is desirable to control carefully what a manager says or expresses even by body language. The wise manager will firstly not attribute faults to individuals when something does not work; he will try and find out 'what' went wrong rather than 'who' made mistakes. Even if any fault is attributed to the behaviour of an official, he should be wise enough not to talk about in a group and certainly not in a large assembly of people. Any public mention of such a faulty action invariably does not serve the real purpose of educating the taker of the action so as to prevent any recurrence. The self-esteem of the person who committed the mistake is hurt, and he may hold a grudge against the speaker even when the speaker is right. If the fault-finder speaker turns out to be wrong, then he will get exposed by the falsely implicated person in the group/assembly itself. If the fault finder is right, all others in the group/assembly may start looking down upon the one who happened to commit that fault. The ability of such a publicly faulted person to get things done from others gets impaired. Typically, Cāṇakya does not say "Do not find fault of others in groups". He only points out that such a person is 'proclaiming' his own fault when he so behaves. Which manager wishes to let others see his own behaviour as faulty? This way of pointing out a behaviour pattern that is best avoided is more likely to work, since we are dealing with capable persons in position of power—the managers.

## 2 आत्मानम् एव नाशयति आत्मवताम् कोपः ।

*ātmānaṁ eva nāśayati ātmavatāṁ kopaḥ*

Anger of the self-esteemed (capable) destroys only themselves.

Anger, whether expressed or not, is a natural instinctive emotion of all human beings, which arises whenever others behave in a way which hurts self-interest or the work at hand. Managers are known to be more prone to anger, because they always have something to get done from others and because disturbances in progress of work are quite common. Getting angry on employees may appear 'to work' and bring the desired result: but experienced managers know that those who always get angry are neither obeyed truly nor are respected. In fact, they may be resented and hated (refer 8.2). But these are effects of anger of a manager on the others – which, he may not be sensitive to, and would not feel strongly about.

The effect of anger on self is more subtle, especially when strong feelings are suppressed. The sequence of events is neatly described as: "Involvement leads to expectations, breaking of expectations leads to anger, anger causes confusion (of thought process), which is turn leads to lack of understanding" (Gita 2.62-63). An angry manager would be somewhat confused when in that state and would tend to interpret things without a total understanding. His conclusions, his decisions and also his resultant actions will be non-appropriate. His effectiveness will be much less and the chances of his failing to achieve his work goals increase substantially. A repeated occurrence of such non-effectiveness would lead to his forfeiting his managerial position. He will get himself 'destroyed' in this way.

The other effect of anger as a strong and persistent emotion is psychosomatic which modern medicine has also confirmed. The risk of persons who are excitable and hot tempered, getting heart attacks is known to be several fold higher. This is a physical destruction of the self.

## 3 न अस्ति अप्राप्यं सत्यव्रताम् !

*na asti a-prāpyaṁ satya-vratāṁ*

Nothing is unachievable for those who keep their promise (word).

A main ingredient in the success of managers or leaders is the trust they have earned amongst their juniors, colleagues and even superiors. The most important trait which ensures such trust generation is keeping their word or promise. A manager who is advised not to find fault with others publicly and not to let anger overtake him is now being told about this good trait. Obviously, to say that 'keeping your word' leads to achievements is not quite correct. But to say that those who keep their promises can attempt to achieve more difficult tasks and are more likely to succeed in it is understandable. The ideas of a trustworthy and trusted manager are more acceptable to those who are to implement them, because the accountability for these ideas will not be shirked by such a manager. His instructions will be also better followed for similar reasons. Thus, achievement of the planned goal will not be difficult for this manager.

4 न केवलेन साहसेन कार्यसिद्धिः भवति ।

*na kevalena sāhasena kārya-siddhiḥ bhavati*

Success in work comes not through daring alone.

Capable persons with multiplicity of resources are naturally inclined to take risks in their efforts for wealth generations. The four elements of management as defined by Cāṇakya – gaining something new, protecting the gained and increasing the protected and even deploying employees – require taking of calculated risks, a certain boldness of action, a little daring attitude. Though such a risk-taking attitude and behaviour is welcome, a caution is sounded here about the inadequacy of daring alone. The five-fold strategising process of *mantra* (3.1) must be followed is the implicit communication here. No impulsive action should be taken even if the opportunity for taking a bold decision arises unexpectedly and suddenly, requiring quick action. This process ensures that at least 2–3 skilled counsellers get involved, and some means of dealing with probable difficulties get planned etc.

Another meaning of *sāhasaṁ* is force (or even violence and cruelty). Force alone does not lead to success is also true. Forcing people to do something out of fear of reprisals etc. would work for some time, but only temporarily. Work results may not be sustainable. However, this meaning *sāhasaṁ* is unlikely to have been meant, considering the following *sūtra*.

5 साहसे खलु श्रीः वसति ।

*sāhase khalu śrīḥ vasati*

Wealth, indeed, resides in risk-taking.

Another version of this *sūtra* has the word *lakṣmi* in place of *śriḥ,* indicating monetary wealth directly.

The risk taking is basic to all wealth generating activities in a society is well-known. All business enterprises – whether agricultural, industrial or services – involve some element of uncertainty, some element of risk. Only those in 'service' of business entrepreneurs have almost no risk. This observation on 'wealth residing in risk-taking' is meant to encourage the manager to take calculated risks in his efforts of wealth generation. The previous *sūtra* has already given the warning that boldness alone will not suffice.

Taking risks means attempting to gain more than otherwise, and also be willing to face failure or semi-success. The gains aimed at may not come through fully, or sometimes, even what would have been achieved without taking the particular risky path, may also get partly lost. The entrepreneur/manager should be willing to accept such losses and still preserve the attitude of risk taking in facing the tasks in future.

This, interestingly, is not an advise of the kind which says 'Take risks to generate wealth'. Cāṇakya seems to be careful in making several suggestions 'indirect', with a view to make his pupils think over them, rather than to take them as directives to be followed blindly.

6 व्यसनार्तः विस्मरति अवश्यकर्तव्यान् ।

*vyasanārtaḥ vismarati avaśya-kartavyān*

(The one) overpowered by vice(s) forgets essential duties.

In an earlier chapter (7.7 to 7.12), consequences of typical vices such as gambling, hunting and lust were mentioned. One more consequence is being spoken about here: forgetting or neglecting to do timely the duties essential for the role that the manager is expected to play. This is another way of stating that the work does not get accomplished (7.7) or properly executed (7.12) or gets neglected (7.9). Why is this *sūtra* given immediately after speaking about risk taking? Perhaps Cāṇakya wanted to emphasise that the manager has to be continuously alert, and must perform all that is necessary at the right time and with proper care. He cannot afford to forget essential 'does and don'ts'. Like the previous *sūtra* this one also is a generalisation connecting cause and effect and the manager has to take the right message from it, namely, carefully avoid getting stuck to vices of any kind.

7 न अस्ति अन्तरायः कालविक्षेपे ।।

*na asti antarāyaḥ kāla-vikṣepe*

There exists no interruption in loss of time.

When one forgets to do the needed jobs, time simply passes away. Time gets lost irretrievably. This statement on how time gets lost is rather startlingly unusual, stating that interruptions do not 'stop' time loss! Almost anything else which one comes across, gets interrupted for one reason or the other. But time is a different entity altogether, and very different from anything else. 'Loss of time' never gets interrupted by itself, without any will of the doer of work during which time is getting lost. Therefore, one needs to be extra careful to ensure that there occurs no time loss, either due to lethargy or due to indecision, or due to non-availability of one or more resources that are needed. The word used by Cāṇakya for 'loss of time' is *kāla-vikṣepaḥ*, not *kāla-kṣepaḥ*. The addition of *vi* indicates not just a passive loss of time but something like deliberately throwing away of time. This emphasis is to demonstrate that such loss of time is controllably by the doer; if it happens to take place, it is tantamount for the doer having done it himself. The doer is not helpless here.

Remembering this *sūtra*, the manager should become an effective time manager who plans work in ways whereby time does not get lost unduly or unnecessarily between work elements or between work stages.

## 8 असंशयविनाशात् संशयविनाशः श्रेयान् ।

*a-saṅśaya-vināśāt saṅśaya-vināśaḥ śreyān*

Better is to eliminate doubt than to continue (to be beset) with it.

The word *saṅśayaḥ* has three sets of meanings which fit here as advice to managers. First is doubt, uncertainty or hesitation. Second is doubt or indecision; and the third is danger, peril or risk.

Managers have to take action when faced with any situation, and most of the times, the information available is neither complete nor fully trustworthy. Doubts arise about the nature of information made available to him, and efforts to get such doubts cleared are necessary. Otherwise, there will arise hesitancy in his actions, because of the uncertainty of the resulting efforts. This kind of hesitancy or unsureness hurts the work being done. Managers, essentially, are men of action: they must decide upon a course of action firmly, whether or not all the information on which they based their decision were to be fully reliable. Of course, they must also foresee the different possible consequences and then be prepared for counteracting the adverse amongst them.

Indecision is a sign of weakness in a manager; it leads to procrastrination invariably, to loss of good opportunities several times and also to vulnerability to mischiefs done by adversaries sometime.

If one sees a danger to the work in hand or a danger to the person involved in a job, it needs no emphasis or even a mention that it is better to remove the danger than not to remove it. However, the danger to the chief as a person is indeed high: it is his power position that is in peril most of the time, and personal safety also not rarely.

Kautiliya Arthaśāstra has paid due attention to the safety of the king, giving ideas on how to protect him even from his sons. Earlier, we have seen a *sūtra* (8.9) which emphatically states that 'Protecting self causes everything to be protected'. Given the political situations in organisations or in nations, this advice on 'removing the dangers' as better than 'to not do so' through unawareness, giving it less importance, or simply for want of timely action, is seen to be very necessary. Those incapable of putting it into action will get removed from their position (or even killed, if circumstances so demand).

In view of the above, Cāṇakya's advice on *saṅśaya-vināśaḥ* needs to be taken in each of the three meanings of the word: uncertainty, indecision and danger.

### *Sūtra* Summary: Managerial Actions

Those who mentions faults of others in assemblies are themselves at fault. Anger destroys those capable persons who get angry. Nothing is unachievable for those who keep promise. Risk taking alone does not make a task succeed; wealth does reside in risk taking.

The vice-ridden forgets essential duties. There exists no uninterruptedness in whiling away time. It is better to eliminate uncertainty/indecision/danger than to live with it.

# CHAPTER 16 ॥ अर्थकामौ ॥ Wealth and Desires

1 केवलं धनानि निक्षेप्तुः न स्वार्थः न दानं न धर्मः ।

*kevalaṁ dhanāni nikṣeptuḥ na svārthaḥ na dānaṁ na dharmaḥ*

For one who just spends away money, it (serves) neither self-interest nor (is it) a payment or a duty.

Having set wealth generation as the primary objective of enterprise management (4.8) and having said that abundance of wealth leads to excellence/prosperity amongst the employees and the society in general (2.1), Cāṇakya now turns to advice on how to use the wealth.

The most readily usable and givable part of wealth-money – needs to be used wisely. The wisdom here consists of using it in such a way that its 'distribution' leads to those receiving it behaving in ways that foster the maintenance and the growth of the organisation/enterprise. Just being liberal with money and giving it away indiscriminately has many undesired consequences of which most managers are keenly aware. Being non-liberal with money, too, leads to dissatisfactions and disaffections amongst employees. The wisdom in giving money is being spelt out here. We will consider the three aspects of using money, in the same order as listed in this *sūtra*: for self, for giving to others, and helping to fulfil ordained duties.

The self-interest expenditure is of three kinds: to satisfy one's own needs and desires, to cater to the desires of the close circle of family and friends, and to ensure that the welfare of employees (all stakeholders of the enterprise) and of the society in general is reasonably taken care of. The first is a short-term satisfaction, the second can be considered medium term in terms of its consequences, while the third really constitutes a long term enlightened self-interest. When the first becomes predominant at the expense of the other two, it is purely and simply selfishness and greed. We recall the earlier *sūtra* (13.7) where an axiomatic statement is made by Cāṇakya. "One who enjoys after satisfying others, enjoys for long time". Given the monarchial system of ruling a kingdom, the likelihood of a king using wealth relentlessly in a selfish manner was very high. So is the likelihood high in a family owned enterprise run authoritatively or when a dictator rules a nation. Therefore, such a statement that "spending money recklessly on oneself is not in self-interest" was needed.

When it comes to payment to near ones or to 'friends', excessive enrichment again, needs to be scrupulously avoided for similar reasons of long term interest of the self, which are almost invariably identical with those of the enterprise or organisation. Nepotism not only stinks, but when exposed and resented by many, leads to the downfall of the executive who is seen to indulge in it.

When money is to be paid out to others, it comes truly under the category of *dāna*. *Dāna* does not mean giving of alms to beggars, or donations to the needy, or offerings to propitiate the god(s). In the context of management, it stands for 'deserved remuneration given without having to be asked for'. Pancatantra[10], which was written around the same time as Arthaśāstra, has beautiful verses on how to nurture employees. Two of them are relevant here.

फलार्थी पार्थिवः लोकान् पालयेत् यत्नम् आस्थितः ।
दानमानादि तोयेन माली मालांकुरान् इव !!

also

राजा तुष्टोऽहि भृत्यानाम् अर्थमात्रं प्रयच्छति ।
ते तु संमानमात्रेण प्राणैः अपि उपकुर्वते ॥

The king desirous of fruits should nurture the people with specific efforts, like a gardener giving water to saplings, he should give them (appropriate) payment and dignity (honour).

The chief, when satisfied (with work), gives at the most money to employees. They, when treated with a little dignity, however, earn his gratefulness by willing to sacrifice even their lives for him.

Giving the right pay with dignity, is a long-term policy which would yield results after long number of years, like a sapling growing into a tree which yields fruits. Management often use 'fair behaviour towards employees' as merely a technique rather than as their basic philosophy. When the expected behaviour change does not take place in a year or two, they revert to their authoritarian pattern. The importance of treating all employees with dignity is brought out effectively in the second verse on loyalty. The word *dāna* as payment stands for this kind of fairness in the amount of pay given and the dignity with which persons are treated (not just as 'hired hands').

In the context of duties assigned to the position of a king, giving money to support appropriate social and cultural causes is also one of them. Several kings became famous because of their monetary support to the learned in various sciences and in philosophy, as well as their nurturing artists such as musicians, dancers and painters. Cāṇakya refers to the fact that indiscriminate spending of money does not serve such a purpose also. In the present context, we may interpret *dharma* of a chief executive of a business enterprise as duties concerned with the societal obligations of his enterprise. This would mean supporting monetarily social and cultural causes which are not directly connected with the 'wealth generating' activity of the enterprise.

## 2 दानं धर्मः ।

*dānaṁ dharmaḥ*

Payment is duty.

Here, the *dānam* is the sense of *vṛtti dānam:* i.e. payment for employment. Fair, timely payment for work is not a favour to be made to the employees: it is in fact the duty of the CEO to ensure that such payment is given. When the employees have to ask for more, it means that either their salary (total remuneration) is not 'fair' – i.e. appropriate for the kind of work they are performing in relation to others, or is not perceived to be fair. Only total transparency in payment policies in relation to the wealth creation activities of the enterprise would lead to elimination of false or inadequate perception of employees on fairness. If a review brings out inadequacy in compensation, it would be fair to correct such lacunae immediately, even with retrospective effect. This kind of attitude towards salary administration is duty: *dānam dharmaḥ.*

Patent unfairness in salary practices, no firm policy structure and adhoc practices – factually or perceived – are most often the cause of large scale dissatisfaction of employees. This is a manifestation of the chief having failed to perform his duty properly.

The common meaning of this *sūtra* is "Giving alms/donations is a (religious) duty"; which is also valid and applicable to all, including to managers in their individual capacity.

## 3 अपरधनानपेक्षं केवलं अर्थदानं श्रेयः ।

*a-para-dhana-anapekṣaṁ kevalaṁ artha-dānaṁ śreyaḥ*

Only that wealth given regardless of the money possessed by others is better.

This is an interesting observation on the process of how wealth – money and other perquisites – tends to be given in a society. Almost invariably, for any work done by a high salaried person, the monetary reward would be much larger to him than to a lowly paid person doing similar work. Even in giving gifts, we tend to give more to the rich and less to the not-so-rich friends of ours! What Cāṇakya advises the CEO is not to fall into this kind of a 'trap'. Payment for work must be independent of the level of richness of the receiver: the payment should reflect the worth of the work itself, rather than that of the receiver! Such payment is 'better' than the payments based on any other consideration except that of the work done.

## 4 न आर्यगतः अर्थवृद्धिपरीतः अनर्थभावः ।

*na ārya-gataḥ artha-vṛddhi-parītaḥ an-artha-bhāvaḥ*

The worthlessness (that arises) from departure of growth in wealth does not behove an honourable person.

This connects with the first *sūtra* (16.1) on throwing away money indiscriminately. When the wealth available is used improperly, the consequences are such that they all lead first to the stoppage of growth of wealth, and then to the erosion of wealth. Once the wealth has left a person, he is not respected in the society and, ultimately, loses his own self-respect. He would then consider himself to be worthless, a feeling that no noble person should find himself subjected to. Here, Cāṇakya is seen to appeal to the self-respect of the managers to dissaude them from being careless in use of money.

5 न्यायागतः अर्थः ।

*nyāya-āgataḥ arthaḥ*

Wealth is (that which is) earned righteously.

The emphasis on ethical means of earning one's livelihood or creating wealth or obtaining resources of any kind is evident here. The word *nyāya* also means decorum, law or justice, virtue, honesty amongst 14 different meanings. All these are different aspects of being ethical in the methods used for creating wealth or for obtaining resources.

6 तद् विपरीतः अर्थाभासः ।

*tad viparītaḥ artha-ābhāsaḥ*

Contrary to that is (only) appearance of wealth.

Together with this *sūtra*, the emphasis on ethics is complete. Any resource or wealth obtained through other than righteous means is only an appearance – it is not to be considered real. This is because appearances are such that any detailed investigation would bring out the illegal or unethical or immoral basis on which this wealth is built. Exposure of this kind invariably leads to destruction of the wealth. It is taken away from the fraudulent owner. The owner of such ill-begotten wealth also loses respect in the society. So, the status that wealth should give its owner is denied to the fraudulent owners.

The CEOs of business enterprises may well memorise this *sūtra* to remind them of the consequences of employing dubious means for short-term gains. Sooner or later, the unethically obtained wealth would dissipate away or lead to bad unbearable consequences.

## 7 यः धर्मार्थौ न पीडयति सः कामः ।

*yaḥ dharma-arthau na pīdayati saḥ kāmaḥ*

That which does not injure duties and resources is (sensual) desire.

In a manner similar to wealth, the pursuit of human desires of all kinds are also meant to be enjoyed following ethical practices. Therefore, this *sūtra* by Cāṇakya specifies clearly which kind of desires are considered acceptable and, therefore, the righteous ones: only those desires, which when being fulfilled, do not come in the way of allotted duties of self and others concerned. (The duties of an individual fall into two distinct categories: ethical and moral. While the ethical duties will be considered to apply universally to all, several moral duties are culture dependant. For example, the family is much more widely interpreted in India than in the USA; and the moral duties towards members of family are many more in India). The gratification of desires should also not lead to reduction in wealth or resources. Any advice on how and how much to enjoy life needs to be given with a clear definition of 'limits' which should not be crossed: here we find a good way of prescribing such limits.

Again, this *sūtra*, though common to all individuals, takes a special importance in the context of a manager, who is entrusted with managing the welfare of many employees. He should not only to set the right example by adhering to these prescribed limits for satisfying his own desires, but should also use this principle to ensure that none of the employees cross the limits to the detriment of others and of the enterprise.

8 तद् विपरीतः कामाभासः ।

*tad vi-parītaḥ kāma-ābhāsaḥ*

Contrary to that is (only) appearance of sensual enjoyment.

Any gratification of desires which keeps the manager away from the duties his role prescribes for him, is not a real enjoyment. It will not only torment his conscience later, but also lead to disaffection amongst his colleagues and juniors, ultimately causing him all kinds of difficulties and unpleasantness. The most dire consequence for this will be forfeiting his position as a manager, which would mean that even the right kind of desires that he has for himself and his family will not get satisfied.

It is this troublesome and temporary nature of desires being gratified – *kāma* – that makes Cāṇakya use the term *ābhasaḥ* or a mere appearance, not reality – to describe the situation.

9 तद् विपरीतः अनर्थसेवी ।

*tad viparītaḥ an-artha-sevī*

Contrary to that gets served with disaster.

When gratification of desires exceeds its bounds, the result is a disaster. We note that in the case of transgressing ethical boundaries while acquiring wealth, such a second statement on what happens as a consequence has not been made by Cāṇakya (He could have worded this *sūtra* 16.9 in *dvi-vacan* like *viparītau* if he had, wanted to refer to both). Clearly, he wants to emphasise the bad consequences of 'wrong' *kāma* more than those of 'wrong' *artha*. Again, in his typical style, he prefers to make an axiomatic statement on bad consequences, rather than telling the manager not to indulge in to excessive sensual gratification.

## 10 अवमानेन आगतं ऐश्वर्यं अवमन्यते साधुः ।

*ava-māanena āgataṁ aisvaryaṁ ava-manyate sādhuḥ*

Prosperity that accrues/comes via loss of self respect is considered lowly by the virtuous.

Another appropriate meanings of the verb *ava-mana* are to decline, to refuse to accept, to feel insulted. In this chapter on wealth and desires, Cāṇakya appeals to the self-esteem of the manager second time, by saying that he will be considered virtuous by others only when the wealth he acquires is without losing his respect, without getting insulted in the process of its acquisition. The reference here is to two distinct types of situations: first is the bad, insulting, undignified treatment at work place and the second is the loss of esteem amongst people when the means of acquisition are unethical and immoral.

It is for both these reasons also, besides the inherent bad consequences of unethical behaviour to the manager and his position, that the manager should take precautions to not accept money where he stands to get humiliated.

Another consequence of virtuous persons not tolerating humiliating circumstances is on the ability of an enterprise - of the CEO – to retain competent persons in the organisation. If the treatment he gives to his juniors, and sometimes even to his senior colleagues, is humiliating, making them lose their self-respect (especially in presence of others), the competent amongst them will quit even when well paid. Only the not-so-competent or the needy will stay on, but will not be motivated to contribute. The two major functions of management then suffer: protecting the gained, and making the protected grow.

**_Sūtra_ Summary: Wealth & Desires**

Spending away money, is neither in self-interest, nor is that (right) payment or duty. Payment is duty. Only that wealth which is given without regard to the richness of the other is preferred. The loss of wealth related feeling of unworthiness does not behove a gentleman. Wealth righteously earned is real wealth; otherwise, it only an apparent wealth. True desires are those which do not hurt either duties or resources, otherwise, it only an appearance of desires, leading to destruction. The virtuous disregards the prosperity achieved through loss of self-respect.

# CHAPTER 17 ॥ चरित्रम् ॥ Character

1 ऋजुस्वभावपरः जनेषु दुर्लभः ।

*ṛju-svabhāva-paraḥ janeṣu dur-labhaḥ*

(A person) totally upright by nature is rare amongst people.

Straightforward, honest and sincere people are rarely to be found. Only by exception would some employee be of this kind, who continues to perform his allotted duties sincerely and would not indulge in politicising at individual or group level. Why has such a statement to be made at all? Two reasons: first, when you find them, give them due recognition and respect, even if they are not so visible or assertive. They are easy to neglect, but over a period of time others will make use of them in a bad way. Second reason is even more important. While the manager should treat all in a fair manner, he should not be naĩve in his trust in others. He ought to look out for behaviour patterns or even simple looking moves of his colleagues and juniors, which can adversely influence the work in hand or the relationships at work. If he notices something amiss, he needs to take suitable corrective actions.

2 गुणवदाश्रयात् निर्गुणः अपि गुणी भवति ।

*guṇavada-aśrayat nir-guṇaḥ api guṇi bhavati*

Serving under the capable, even the incapable becomes capable.

The capabilities inherent in a person are almost invariably underestimated, both by himself and by others, especially, by his superiors. Those managers who complain of not getting the right persons to work with need to recognise the truth behind this statement. We are familiar with the 'Pigmallion Effect', where a flower girl got transformed into a lady. This *sūtra* conveys essentially that kind of a message. An interesting verse from Pancatantra on capability is:

अश्वः शस्त्रं शास्त्रं वाणी वीणा नरश्च नारीच ।
पुरुषविशेषं प्राप्ता भवन्ति अयोग्याश्च योग्याश्च ॥

Horse, weapon, science, speech, violin, man and women,
On reaching a specific person, become either suitable or unsuitable.

A good manager, therefore, should strive to retain good, capable person who in turn will train others to become capable.

As a corollary, if too many juniors are being seen as not capable enough, their supervisor needs to be looked at carefully. If he is not giving enough attention to improve the capabilities of his men, he should be alerted on this aspect of his responsibility.

## 3 क्षीराश्रितम् जलम् क्षीरम् एव भवति ।

*kṣīraśritaṁ jalaṁ kṣīraṁ eva bhavati*

Water, having reached milk, becomes milk, itself.

A metaphor to emphasise the fact of capability getting spread. However, this metaphor does not really fit. The process of water getting the whiteness of milk does not involve any 'effort' by the milk. The whitening – becoming milk like – happens automatically. Obviously, just being near or serving a capable would not so automatically improve an incapable person.

## 4 महात्मना परेण साहसं न कर्तव्यम् ।

*mahātmana pareṇa sāhasaṁ na kartavyaṁ*

A noble person ought not make another to act in risk affair.

A magnanimous or a noble person should lead from the front, when it comes to taking risks. This attitude is ingrained in the officers of the army, but not necessarily in managers of enterprises. The risky affairs in business, unlike those in defence services, are not physical. The risks are to the successful completion of work. These can be of different kinds: non- performance of deployed workers, uncertainty of decisions taken in the absence of full information etc. The accountability for such risks-that is, the resultant unfavourable outcomes, must not be put by the manager on others. He should give credit to others for success in risky endeavours, but own responsibility for non-success. A major advantage of such attitude is that the manager himself will keep a thorough control on the work as it progresses, and use his wisdom to take care of difficulties as they arise. The chances of successful accomplishment increase substantially in this way. Moreover, his team is motivated to share the risk and to think flexibly, resulting in better loyalty to the boss and to the organisational goals.

## 5 कदाचित् अपि चरित्रं न लंघयेत् ।

*kadācit api caritraṁ na laṅghayet*

Not even once should (one) transgress character.

The verb *laṅgh* in its causative sense also means to violate or to destroy. Any violation or transgression of the character – which is always used in the sense of good character – leads to its destruction. The character of a person, a manager, is the image that he has assiduously built over years in the minds of the people with whom he interacts socially and professionally. This image is a result of a large number of actions that he has taken, the responses that he has given to the multifaceted situations he has faced during all the years that have formed his past. Such behaviour establishes a pattern which makes his future actions predictable in the sense of their objectives. A manager with a good character, for example, will be expected to be fair and just, in dealing with juniors. It is not meaningful to predict exactly what action he would take in any situation: it suffices to be sure about the nature of the action. If a manager with such a reputation about his character were to suddenly turn vindictive, that would be a transgression, a violation of his character.

Even for the managers with excellent character, circumstances can arise where pressure gets built-up or is exerted to tempt him to do something unethical that he would normally not do. That is why this directive by Cāṇakya: "Do not cross the limits".

## 6 क्षुधार्तः न तृणं चरति सिंहः ।

*kṣudhārtaḥ na tṛṇaṁ carati siṁhaḥ*

A lion suffering hungerpangs does not eat grass.

The emphasis on not transgressing the character is exemplified through this metaphor. The most severe pressure that gets exerted on a living entity is the non-availability of food. Hunger, intense hunger pains are known to drive a person to eat anything which he would normally not eat at all – just as a lion does not eat grass. For a meat eater lion, a vegetarian grass diet is below his dignity, outside his character. Just as a lion will not transgress under intense pressure, so should a manager hold to his character.

## 7 प्राणात् अपि प्रत्ययः रक्षितव्यः ।

*prāṇat ap pratyayaḥ rakṣitavyaḥ*

Confidence/Trust ought to be protected even with life.

A manager with a strong and virtuous character should be prepared to stake his life itself, if it comes to retaining the trust people have given him. If he has promised that he will do something, which is another meaning of *pratyayah,* he should certainly do it even if the task becomes very difficult or dangerous. *Pratyayaḥ* also means fame, renown or reputation. The reputation of the manager is really at stake. Once he loses it then to regain the reputation or trust of the employees and the employers becomes very difficult. A saying of this type as the *Raghu-kul-rīti* is well known throughout the Indian subcontinent.

## 8 पिशुनः नेता पुत्रदारैः अपि त्यज्यते ।

*piśunaḥ neta putra-daraiḥ api tyajyate*

A malignant leader is forsaken even by the wives and sons.

The relevant meanings of the word *piśunaḥ* are: slanderous, backbiting, hard, unkind, wicked, malignant, low, vile, and stupid, foolish. All seem to apply well in this *sūtra*. The point being made by Cāṇakya is that when a leader is or becomes non-virtuous or in-capable, even those close to him will distance themselves from his bad actions, and ultimately leave him. To expect support from even family members is not possible for those who leave the path of virtue.

## 9 बालात् अपि अर्थजातम् श्रुणुयात् ।

*bālat api artha-jātaṁ śruṇayāt*

When full of meaning, even the (saying) from an ignoramous ought to be listened to.

One of the characteristics of a virtuous person is the in-built humility, and the consequent willingness to listen to the others. Also, a well groomed manager has trained himself to pay due respect to all others and to consider their views. Often, the outsider, the non-knowledgeable or a simple person who does not play politics, asks questions or makes comments which throw an entirely different light on the situation. Such remarks can many a times help to take more effective actions for successful completion of the task at hand. It is for such reasons, that this *sūtra* has been formulated. Remarks of the not so wise, help directly or indirectly, if well used.

## 10 सत्यम् अपि अश्रद्धेयम् न वदेत् ।

*satyaṁ api a-śraddheyaṁ na vadet*

The un-believable, even when true, should not be spoken.

This is a rather surprising advice, when all are expected to be truthful, especially those managers who are renowned for their good character. A self-righteous manager, since he knows that others know him to be one, is likely to be careless when he is conveying facts. Cāṇakya warns him to be careful, to think through from the others' point of view, and then to desist from speaking out if the listeners are unlikely to believe in what he is going to say.

Such a non-belief, disbelief or a total rejection of the statement by the listeners can take place for many reasons which have nothing to do with the predictability of the manager per se. If the statement is against any strong, deep-rooted belief of the listeners, rejection becomes natural. This would result in eroding the credibility of the speaker-manager.

If it is necessary to convey such a difficult to believe but true statement, the manager must collect enough incontrovertible proof in support of his statement. And he should be prepared to prove his case. When this can be done, the statement to be made is no more of the incredible kind, since proof can be cited. But the presentation of the facts would need to be done skilfully in such a way to get the listeners to accept the proof as valid, and thereafter, accept the unpalatable fact.

### *Sūtra* Summary: Character

Persons of upright nature are rare. The incapable become capable in the company of capable persons. Water, when mixed with milk, becomes milky. An honourable person should not let other to take a risk on his behalf. One should not transgress one's character. A hungry lion does not eat grass. Trust must be protected even by staking one's life. A wicked leader is dropped even by wives and sons. One should listen even to an ignorant person if he says something meaningful. Truth, if not believable, better not be told.

CHAPTER

# 18 ॥ दोषाः ॥ Faults

1 बहून् अपि गुणान् एकदोषः ग्रसति ।

*bahūn api guṇān ek-doṣaḥ grasati*

Many a virtues are eclipsed by a single fault.

When judging people, the manager has to consider their total character, good points as well as their faults. This *sūtra* states that when a major fault exists in the character of a person, it has a very profound deleterious effect on his performance and also in his behaviour. This effect is so large that it overshadows all the good characteristics he possess. Neither his skills not his knowledge in different areas become effective at work, and, therefore, he cannot be trusted to accomplish the given work successfully.

2 न अल्पदोषात् बहुगुणाः त्यज्यन्ते ।

*na alpa-doṣat bahu-gunaḥ tyajyante*

For a minor fault, many good qualities are not sacrificed/forsaken.

Having pointed out that a major fault overshadows many a good qualities, promptly follows the next *sūtra* about a minor fault. A minor deficiency often becomes too visible, and several good qualities get revealed only when faced with circumstances where those are needed. A manager, consequently tends to notice faults easily but does not perceive the good qualities that his juniors and colleagues – even his boss – possess. He then selects persons for tasks on the basis of such a faulty perception of reality. Thus, persons with good qualities important for the job at hand may get rejected owing to their having exhibited a minor deficiency. Hence this warning to the manager about how to look at faults and virtues appropriately while selecting the right person for the right job.

## 3 विपश्चित्सु अपि सुलभाः दोषाः ।

*vipścitsu api sulabhaḥ doṣāḥ*

Faults, are easily found even amongst the learned.

Human beings are naturally not perfect. Even after all the training is imparted in philosophy, sciences, morality, and in skills etc., the result is not expected to be perfect – a fact which every teacher and every trainer is painfully aware of. Even so, there exists a tendency to attribute all good qualities to the learned, keeping them on a 'high pedastal'. Then follows the disappointment that they have 'feet of clay'! Cāṇakya wants his management trainees to be absolutely clear, that faults exists even in the accomplished persons that he will encounter. 'Expect such situation, and be prepared to deal with it appropriately' is the message here.

## 4 न अस्ति रत्नम् अखण्डितम् ।

*na asti ratnam a-khaṇditam*

No precious stone is without a crack.

A metaphor to emphasise that no one is perfect. Not even the most valued person, who possesses many good qualities, and who has many accomplishments to his credit can be entirely free of faults or deficiencies.

5 मर्यादातीतम् न कदाचित् अपि विश्वसेत् ।

*maryādā-atītaṁ na kadācit api viśvaset*

Never even once trust one who has crossed the limit.

In judging (people) employees in the context of work, trust forms a major ingredient. Can this person be trusted to be sincere to the given assignment, to be able to seek guidance or to resolve difficulties on his own, to be able to accomplish the task, once delegated, without supervision? Several such questions get answered positively based on the previous work record of the person. One item that is commonly likely to escape attention is the behaviour of the person while getting things done. If he is seen to have 'crossed limits' he better not be trusted, even though he may be otherwise capable. The limits here would refer to interpersonal behaviour and to ethical considerations taken together. If he hurts people, trodding on their toes; or snatches away credit from others; or uses undue force to pressurise juniors; or manipulates situations to coerce colleagues etc., then he better not be trusted. Crossing of ethical limits within and outside the organisation is of many kinds, and is fairly well known and understood.

6 अप्रिये कृते प्रियम् अपि द्वेष्यम् भवति ।

*a-priye kṛte priyaṁ api dveṣyaṁ bhavatī*

Even the good done to the disliked becomes hateworthy.

At workplaces of all kinds, when many individuals work together, likes and dislikes for individuals do arise inevitably. Some gel together, some cannot see eye to eye; such a situation is usually managed by insisting that when working together as a team on a task, liking each other is desirable but not necessary. One learns to keep away personal likes and dislikes from affecting adversely the team processes and the work goals. However, managers do need to take steps to eliminate discords, and also to make persons who have developed a dislike for him to shed such dislike. The principle propounded in this *sūtra* recommends that it is not advisable 'to do a good turn' to such a person: instead of eliminating dislike, it will get fostered, even to the stage of enmity. This is because that person would see through the move, interpret it as an attempt to buy him over, and resolve even more strongly not to succumb to such manipulation.

Obviously, other means of removing the discord need to be explored for making such a person dislike the manager - another person – less.

## 7 नमन्ति अपि तुलाकोटिः कूपोदकक्षयं करोति ।

*namanti api tulākotiḥ kūpa-udaka-kṣayaṁ karoti*

Though bowing (polite), the pot-wheel empties away well water.

Yet another metaphor, appropriate to that time; but does not seem to convey the right meaning with reference to the preceding *sūtra*. Incidentally, the dictionary meanings of the word *tula-koti* do not fit here. Is his *sūtra* a non-authentic insertion?

8 सताम् मतम् न अतिक्रमेत् ।

*satam matam na ati-kramet*

Opinion of the truthful (good persons) should not be transgressed.

The upright, saintly persons would normally not be interested in making the manager or others behave in ways beneficial to themselves, at the cost of the task or of the organisation. They would, however, be assertive enough to express their opinions and views candidly, transparently. They would not rebel if such an opinion is not listened to or corresponding actions are not taken. Therefore, their opinions are likely to be considered worthy of benign neglect. The manager better not fall into this trap, warns Cāṇakya. Not giving due attention to their view or even flouting the advice given by them, would invite trouble and difficulties for the organisation. However unpalatable or away from the mainstream thinking such opinions may appear, these should be given due consideration.

**Sūtra Summary: Faults**

Many a good qualities are overshadowed by a major fault. Many good qualities are not forsaken for a small fault. Faults are easy to find even in the learned. No precious stone is without a crack. Never ever trust a person who has crossed limits. Even favours made to the disliked person become cause of hatred. Though bowing down, the pot wheel empties the well of water. Opinion of the virtuous should not be neglected.

# CHAPTER 19 ॥ उत्साहः ॥ Enthusiasm

1 उत्साहवताम् शत्रवः अपि वशीभवन्ति ।

*utsāha-vatām śatravaḥ api vaśī-bhavanti*

For the enthusiastic, even enemies become favourable.

By now, in the 185 *sūtras* of the first 18 chapters, Cāṇakya has asked so many different things to be done (and not to be done), that we start wondering how the would be manager can really implement them all. But reality, in fact, is even more complicated and the one quality that is needed above all is *utsāhaḥ* – a word which has many different meanings, all of which make sense for the managers role: effort, exertion; energy; perseverance, one for the three *śakti* (capabilities/powers) of a ruler, the other two being *mantra* and *prabhava*; determination, resolution; power, ability; firmness, fortitude, strength; and (in rhetoric) firmness/fortitude which gives rise to heroic sentiment; and lastly, happiness.

Indeed, a tremendous amount of energy, strength and perseverance over long periods of time is needed, which can all come only with a basically healthy body and mind. This is also a major reason for advocating absence from vices and adherence to ethics in true spirit.

For persons endowed with this kind of enthusiasm – *utsāhaḥ* – it is not only easy to motivate friends, but also to convert adversaries and enemies into supporters of his cause. The performance of the enthusiastic manager speaks for itself, gradually melting the negatives in the minds of the opposition. Such a manager, innately optimistic, will ensure that he does not directly criticise or offend his opponents in personal terms. He will find time to think through ways of winning them over to the cause, and will have the perseverance to implement such ways gradually over time.

2 विक्रमधनाः हि राजानः ।

*vikrama-dhanāḥ hi rajanāḥ*

Prowess, indeed, is the richness of (kings) chiefs.

Top managers need to possess strengths which people normally do not. In fact, in many different situations, the leader has to demonstrate his prowess dramatically, with a dash of dare-devilry. Heroism is indeed seen as a big ingredient in the make-up of strong and effective leaders.

So Cāṇakya goes on to define the chiefdom itself in terms of heroism. Those enriched with prowess/heroism are leaders.

We note that the 'manager' or the 'administrator' (the ruler) envisaged by Cāṇakya is a 'leader' in the sense this word is used in management today. Since management has been defined entrepreneurily as gaining, protecting and growing the gained, it is understandable that the manager's role as described is that of leader-manager.

3 न अस्ति अलसस्य ऐहिकं आमुष्मिकं वा ।

*na asti alasasya aīhikaṁ āmūṣmikaṁ vā*

For the lazy, is neither this world nor the next (after death).

The opposite of *utsāhaḥ* is *alasaḥ*, in every single sense. In Chapter 4 on Management, we first come across this word in the context of even the capable and the strong person with friends will not attempt to gain something new (4.4 to 4.6) etc. In this *sūtra* coming after describing the need for enthusiasm and heroism, is a clear warning: absence of *utsāhaḥ* is not status quo, but it is a 'gone case'. Even that which is available will be lost soon enough. That is how ''here is nothing' for a lazy person in this world. Cāṇakya also threatens the leader manager, that even in the heaven he will be devoid of all goods: a threat which would work well on the believers (understandably, he does not speak of hell!).

## 4 निरुत्साहात् दैवम् पतति ।

*nir-utsāhāt daivaṁ patati*

From lack of enthusiasm, chance (of success) reduces.

Luck favours only those who put in lots of right efforts with zeal, even god helps only those who help themselves! This *sūtra* says the same thing by way of a generalisation. The chances of success-the probability of obtaining the desired result-fall down, get reduced when there is lack of enthusiasm needed to ensure perseverance of efforts.

In the *sūtra* 10.5 a similar idea was expressed by saying that luck follows efforts. At the same time, 10.6, 11.7, it is recognised that sometimes tasks undertaken become difficult to achieve due to luck not being in favour of success. With the present axiomatic statement, Cāṇakya emphasises that lack of perseverance will always reduce the chance of success. One more reason to maintain enthusiasm in all actions, no matter how many difficulties arise in the course of work.

5 आत्मच्छिद्रम् न प्रकाशयेत् ।

*ātma-cchidraṁ na prakāśayet*

One ought not publicise/reveal own vulnerability.

A little loss of enthusiasm can lead to some pessimism, which in turn could result into blaming oneself for the non-achievement. In such a negative mood, even an accomplished manager starts discovering lacunae in himself (not in the basis or in the means or in the efforts!), some real and some apparent. If such an introspection leads to diagnosing the real deficiency and then to removing it, that is good, as it should be. But if this manager starts brooding and dwelling upon some particular weakness, he is likely to reveal it to others, seeking relief in a cathartic release. He should better not do so, is the advice. Exposing own weakness does not help reducing it, but may lead to undesirable consequences.

6 छिद्रप्रहरणः शत्रवः अपि ।

*chhidra-praharaṇaḥ śatravaḥ api*

Those hitting on vulnerable spots are indeed adversaries.

One major consequence is that the manager will be hit where found vulnerable. This is for certain. In fact, one major strength without which any person cannot survive for long in a power position is absence of any vulnerability. Most bold decisions taken in the interest of the organisation or of success at work are such that the vested interest of some employee or of some employee group are adversely affected. At such times the bold new move can be effectively stalled by hitting at the vulnerable spot of the chief who calls the shots. Such persons, who use weakness to hit a manager are certainly his adversaries or downright enemies. A true friend will identify the weakness and help the chief to remove it or to reduce its possible bad affects.

## 7 स्वजनस्य दुर्वृत्तम् निवारयेत् ।

*swa-janasya dur-vṛttaṁ nivārayet*

Wrong behaviour of own persons should be reformed.

The enthusiasm of the top management is often marred by the mis-deeds of the persons close to them, or by persons at the higher levels of hierarchy. Such misdeeds can be overt or covert, intentional or unintentional, acts of commission or omission; but their adverse impact on others' behaviour and on the conduct of work in hand is much larger than a similar inappropriate behaviour by others not so close to the top. This *sūtra* implies that the chief should not be under the impression that his team (and family members) will always behave in a manner supporting the cause. He should be aware – and be wary – that wrong behaviour can occur. He should look for it carefully, and if found, undertake salvage operations immediately. One part is counselling the person about this piece of behaviour, showing the adverse consequences and asking for change in the right direction. Force should be used to the extent needed. The other part is to take care of the impact of wrong actions already taken by calling those affected, explaining reality, making midcourse corrections for the unexpected deviations that have crept in etc.

## 8 एकाङ्गदोषः पुरुषम् अवसादयति !

*eka-anga-doṣaḥ puruṣaṁ ava-sādayati*

The fault of on-sidedness causes a man to get destroyed.

Energetic persons can get fixed on a specific idea or plan of theirs to such an extent that they can become blind to peripheral areas. They would then fail to see some unexpected changes that have come about; or would simply be unable to listen to divergent views of team members. Their concentration on the idea itself then becomes a fault. Such a fault then leads to failure, which in turn would lead to the manager losing his position or job. Another situation arises when a person is affected with a major fault, which he perhaps recognises, but cannot help himself. Infatuation with a woman, or strong addiction to gambling etc. could be such faults. Even behavioural faults such as excessive anger or excessive hesitation cum indecision etc. can also lead to a manager's downfall.

## 9 कम् अपि पुरुषम् न अवमन्येत ।

*kam api puruṣaṁ na ava-manyeta*

One ought not belittle (or insult) any person whatever.

Many a managers, when they are annoyed at a junior arguing his case or defending himself while explaining some work failure, are tempted to "show the blighter his place". Some managers are rude in their treatment of juniors sometimes deliberately, or as matter of useful stance to get things done. Some times, in anger or as an instantaneous reaction, insults are hurled on the juniors for their perceived inappropriate work behaviour. In every such instance, the junior feels be-littled and gets hurt. Even body language used hurts in a similar way. Such hurts get remembered over long time periods, accumulate, and then lead to work disturbances and also to rebellion against the manager. Such managers also lose respect of colleagues and other juniors. Therefore, this injunction: better not belittle any one, whatever his relative position in the hierarchy.

If a manager needs to be so much in control of himself when dealing with persons within the organisation, he would need to be more careful when dealing with other stakeholders such as suppliers, customers, financers etc. This edict applies to all persons which he comes in contact with, including amongst family and friends.

This *sūtra* is somewhat differently worded from the earlier one on 'harsh speech' (8.1). Cruelty in speech is only one form of insulting a person: a manager has too many different ways available to belittle his juniors or even a colleague. He needs to be aware of the way in which his actions, speech, and body language can be interpreted to mean an insult to them by the listeners. And people are known to be very differently sensitive in such matters as well as in the candidness of their 'feedback' to the boss about how bad they felt at that time point. It is, therefore, for the manager to develop a good understanding of such situations and then to prepare himself for taking the right corrective actions. Retrieval, as most managers know, is possible in an overwhelming majority of un-meant offences of belittling others.

10 क्षन्तव्यं इति पुरुषम् न बाधेत ।

*kṣantavyaṁ iti puruṣaṁ na badheta*

(Considering) May be pardoned, (one) should not be vindictive against any person.

The advice given in the previous *sūtra* is followed up by saying that the misbehaviour of juniors that possibly led to the manager's anger should be pardoned. The person should not be hurt because of it. We see here that the pardon is not for the person, it is for his behaviour. Knowing that human beings are fallible, and that mistakes or even misdemeaners occur often because of non-understanding or faulty understanding, any such inappropriate behaviour needs to be corrected. And the manager should do it without unduly hurting the ego of the person at fault.

Employees sometime commit errors of omission or commission owing to their faulty understanding of the organisational politics If their moves are seen or perceived to be against himself by their boss, he needs to be extra careful. Hurting the ego of such a junior, who may be getting used as a pawn by an adversary, can prove very troublesome. It is better to act in such a way that the political move gets neutralised and the junior again begins to act in a politically right manner to help the work on hand succeed.

The patience and the perseverance needed for such actions are shown only by the energetic and strong managers.

11 कार्यसंकटेषु अर्थव्यवसायिनी बुद्धिः ।

*kārya-saṅkateṣu artha-vyavasāyinī buddhiḥ*

Intelligence is that which uses resources (meaningfully) for resolution of difficulties in work.

A skill that a manager needs to posses is the ability to use the available resources appropriately to resolve difficulties that arise in any work. As a fourth part of the process of strategising every new work – *mantra,* we have seen earlier that a manager should anticipate difficulties and plan for their resolution (*vinipāta-pratīkāraḥ*). However much a manager plans in advance, unexpected difficulties do occur. Therefore, a manager needs to be trained to consider what all resources he has, which of them are likely to be useful, in which way such use can be done, and what would be the result. He must also be prepared for some side-effects of the proposed action. This capability to deal with the unexpected difficulties will gradually strengthen through experience. He would learn from successes as well as failures. Introspection after failure is the fastest teacher, provided the exercise is done in a detached manner. Any self-justifying exercise which blames others or events does not teach anything to the egostic manager who is out to defend himself.

### *Sūtra* Summary: Enthusiasm

Enthusiasts can convert even enemies into supporters. Prowess, indeed, is the richness of chiefs. The lazy deserve neither this world nor the next. Without enthusiasm, the chance of success recedes. Own vulnerability should not be revealed; those who strike at weaknesses are adversaries. Inappropriate behaviour of near ones should be corrected. One sidedness is a fault that destroys a man. One should not belittle any person whatever. Pardon wrong aets, do not become vindictive against a person. Good intelligence is that which helps resolve work difficulties.

# CHAPTER 20 ॥ स्वजनः ॥ Own Persons

1 स्वजनेषु अतिक्रमः न कर्तव्यः ।

*swa-janeṣu ati-kramaḥ na kartayaḥ*

Do not cross limits (or neglect) in the cases of near ones/own persons.

The near ones tend to be taken for granted. In the case of a chief or the CEO, the near ones are the (family) relatives amongst employees and also those who constitute his close circle of advisers. In the case of a king (and rarely in the case of a family held business enterprise) even the family members acquire 'un-constitutional power' owing to their perceived ability to influence decisions to be taken by the king. And these persons who are close to him are his 'own persons'. He ought not to transgress limits when dealing with them is Cāṇakya's advice. This advice comes even after the earlier *sūtra* (19) adjoining him not to belittle any one. This is because of two reasons: we feel like taking liberties with the near ones. "They will know I do not have bad intentions for them" etc. is the attitude. But this may not work. Secondly, and more importantly, when hurt by any transgression, the close ones will retaliate much more vehemently, when they get an opportunity. In fact, they will not only keep looking for such opportunities for revenge, but also help creating them. They are, after all, better placed to initiate political harm.

2 माता अपि दुष्टा त्याज्या ।

*mātā api duṣṭā tyājyā*

Even the mother should be forsaken, if vile/viscious/ corrupted.

The other side of this good advice on not to transgress limits with near ones, is to treat them as their behaviour and actions deserve, when they create trouble. Taking a lenient view because of their nearness is definitely not recommended. To bring out this aspect with clarity and force, Cāṇakya brings in this *sūtra* the most revered 'near person' in the world for any one – including for the manager: one's own mother. If she turns out to be vile, or becomes viscious for some reason, if she gets under the influence of her near ones and joins harmful plots etc., she should be removed to a position where she cannot harm. Even the mother must be abandoned or expelled from her place in the family, to ensure that no harm comes through her. Firm and ruthless actions of this kind against the errant near ones does require a considerable amount of *indriya-jaya*, which only a *jit-ātma* can exercise.

3 स्वहस्तः अपि विषदिग्धः छेद्यः ।

*swa-hastaḥ api viṣa-digdhaḥ chedyaḥ*

Own hand also worthy of being cut off, when imbibed with poison.

This metaphor which every surgeon who has amputated a gangrene afflicted limb is familiar with, describes the situation well. If timely action is not taken, the poison that has entered the body system through bad elements will spread, making it fatal to the body.

Like surgeons prefer amputing a poisoned arm to save the body, the organisation must be protected by separating out the bad element, especially when a very close one.

4 अप्रतीकारेषु अनादरः न कर्तव्यः ।

*a-pratīkāreṣu anādaraḥ na kartavyaḥ*

One ought not disrespect those who do not desist (or oppose).

Every manager knows from his experience that employees, including those in the close circle, are of three kinds. First are those who understand and follow properly the work plans, since they agree with all steps planned. The second are those who do not like what is proposed and openly oppose the steps until they are convinced. The third type is passive; they may not be in full agreement, but they do not oppose. Their presence is not felt strongly, but their discomfort can be noticed if looked for. It is this third kind of persons who are likely to get neglected, or be subjected to downright disrespect which can manifest itself in several ways. Cāṇakya advises the manager not to fall into this type of a situation. Those who do not show opposition can be strong willed, and if shown disrespect over a period of time, can revolt overtly or covertly. They can also start sabotaging the work being done by the chief. Such persons should not be underestimated. Their positive support is worth preserving and their nuisance value is high.

Apparently, in this *sūtra* and the next few, Cāṇakya is drawing attention to some items which are not normally followed by the enthusiastic and perseverant managers, due to their engrossment in the task at hand.

5 परः अपि च हितः बन्धुः ।

*paraḥ api ca hitaḥ bandhuḥ*

If an outsider/foreigner is benevolent, he too is a friend/brother.

The definition of a foreigner or an outsider is not just geographical; the nearness or friendliness is more to be decided upon by the behaviour of the person. His intentions – vocalised or not – are to be interpreted by the nature of his actions. If the actions are supportive or favourable to the cause of the manager, then such outsiders are to be considered close and useful like a brother or a friend.

6 गुणे न मत्सरः कर्तव्यः ।

*guṇe na matsaraḥ kartavyaḥ*

No jealousy ought to be shown in virtue.

Good qualities in a person are an asset to himself and to the organisation to which he belongs. Such qualities have either put him in high positions or are likely to lead him to such positions. Those who do not possess such qualities amongst his colleagues and juniors are, therefore, likely to feel jealous of the person and of his qualities. Jealousy of this type is not the right thing to do: it is better to strive for acquiring the quality which is missing. The chief needs to keep this in mind and to discourage jealousy amongst his people by suitable means. Of course, the chief himself should not be jealous of good qualities amongst his colleagues and juniors. His self-esteem should not depend on such relative judgements.

7 संसदि शत्रुं न परिक्रोशेत् ।

*saṅsadi śatruṁ na pari-krośet*

Enemy is not to be lamented upon in an assembly.

This edict is similar to the earlier one on good behaviour expected in assemblies (15.1) "Do not describe faults of others". Here, the reference is specifically to adversaries or enemies. What purpose, after all, is served by either lamenting upon what they are doing or are likely to do? Even denouncing the enemy and thereby getting others to agree to it does not change the reality in any way. If one has a plan to overcome the adverse effects of enemy actions, better to form a small group to give a good shape to such a plan" *mantra-mūlāḥ sarva-ārambhāḥ* (All tasks begin with strategising: 3.1). If a leader only talks about the enemy's actions in an assembly, he is exposing the fact that he is hurt, but has no means to counteract. Better not do so is the advice.

8 शत्रोः अपि सुगुणाः ग्राह्याः ।

*śatroḥ api suguṇāḥ grāhyāḥ*

Good qualities are worth acquiring even from the enemy.

Emotions cloud judgement when enmity exists between two persons or parties. "Everything that the enemy does must be bad for me/us and so the enemy cannot possibly have any good qualities" is the feeling that can get generated. One of the major components of the advice to the leader-manager on becoming a *jitātma* (one who has conquered himself) is to be able to prevent strong negative emotions such as jealousy, anger, enmity from occupying the mindspace. When these emotions are under control, it is easier to assess not only the colleagues but also the enemies reasonably objectively. Then the leader sees good qualities in all, including in his enemies. Such good qualities are worth emulating.

## 9 चिरपरिचितानाम् अत्युपचारः शंकितव्यः ।

*cira-paricitanāṁ ati-upacāraḥ śankitavyaḥ*

Excessive obeisance from those familiar since long is to be doubted.

Leaders exhibit heroism and so are admired, and worshipped by all. They get accustomed to being in such a position. A warning is given here by Cāṇakya to them. Of the 17 different meanings of the word *upacārah* those relevant here are four: worship; civility, politeness; flattery, compliments; and salutation or customary obeisance. If any of the person in the familiar circle starts showing excess in any of these four kinds of behaviour, the leader should start doubting the motive behind it. Why this change? What is he hiding or wanting to start or wishing to ask for in near future? Answer to such questions need to be found and appropriate steps taken.

## 10 अतिसंगः दोषम् उत्पादयाति ।

*ati-saṅgaḥ doṣaṁ utpādayati*

Excessive closeness generates fault.

The man at the top of any hierarchy is lonely. He may find relief in one or two close relationships with senior colleagues or outsider friends. This is undesirable, because it will always have adverse repercussions. One of the close persons may be tempted to misuse the relationship. Others will wonder 'why' such relationship and attribute non-existing bad motives. They will also form an impression that the leader is under the influence of these close individuals, that such influence will not be for the good of the organisation or its goal. The ethical and moral righteousness of the leader will be questioned, even if no deviation from the good path is seen to take place.

The same reasoning also holds good for managers at all levels of hierarchy. Managers are therefore advised not to permit any person to become too close to themselves, in the interest of the organisation.

### *Sūtra* Summary: Own Persons

Do not overstep limits in relations to the near ones. Even the mother, if viscious, should be forsaken. Own hand ought to be cut off if infested with poison. One should not disrespect those who do not oppose. A benevolent outsider is, of course, a supporter. Virtue (in others) should not lead to jealousy (in self). Enemy is not to be denounced in assemblies. Good qualities of even the enemy are worth acquiring. Excessive flattery from the long familiar persons is to viewed with suspicion. Excessive closeness generates fault.

# CHAPTER 21 ॥ धर्मः ॥ Ethics

1 धर्मेण धार्यते लोकः ।

*dharmeṇa dhāryate lokaḥ*

The world is supported/looked after through ethics.

The root meaning of '*dharma*' is 'that which supports'. An emphatic statement on 'how' is found in Maha-bharata[11]. न राज्यं न च राजा अपि न दण्डो न च दाण्डिकाः । धर्मेण इव प्रजाः सर्वाः रक्षन्ति हि परस्परम् । *Na rājyaṁ na ca rāja api, na daṇdo na ca dāṇdikāḥ, dharmeṇa iva prajāḥ sarvaḥ rakṣanti hi parasparaṁ.* "Neither the kingdom, nor the king; not law, nor the police, only through ethical behaviour do all the people protect each other."

Truly, a civilised society is possible only because we are all taught to protect each other by following the biblical dictum of "Do unto others what you would want them to do unto you". It is with this background that the above *sūtra* states that ethics must be used by the (king) CEO to ensure appropriate behaviour of the employees, and of the other stakeholders including the society. Behaviour deviating from ethical/moral norms needs to be curbed, with use of appropriate means, including force.

2 दया धर्मस्य जन्मभूमिः ।

*dayā dharmasya janma-bhūmiḥ*

Empathy is the motherland of ethics.

Sympathy for others in trouble or in deprived circumstances, without their having committed any immoral or unethical act, is not as 'natural' as one would wish to believe. The self preserving instincts of a thinking animal that the human being is, often turns into pure selfishness irrespective of the cost to others or aloof from the misery of other humans in the same society. Civil society, therefore, nurtures a sense of sympathy for fellow humans. The more we learn to empathise with others, the more we feel like working towards removing conditions that create manmade deprivations for others. Ethical behaviour, which respects the feelings of others with the same strength as our own, is prompted by such a feeling of empathy. It is in this sense that empathy is the mother (note, not the father!) land of ethics. Only in the fertile ground of empathy can the seeds of ethical behaviour grow into trees that blossom.

3 धर्ममूले सत्यदाने ।

*dharma-mūle satya-dāne*

Truth and payment, both are rooted in ethics.

Why do we consider speaking the truth or behaving truthfully as 'good' behaviour, as a virtue to be imbibed from childhood and to be nourished and adhered to lifelong? Only because when a non-truth or a downright untruth is used for any kind of 'gain' by an individual, the 'gain' is at the expense of someone else. A similar non-truthful action from the affected individual is not welcome. That precisely is the proposition of ethics: "If A's behaviour affecting B makes A happy, replacing A by B should not change the situation." So truthfulness is rooted in ethics.

*Dāna*, as stated earlier, is not only alms and donations, but also *vṛtti-dāna*, i.e. payment for work. All three stem from empathy, the birthplace of ethics. Fairness in payment for work is ethics, i.e. paying as much the job is worth, taking account of the job content aspects as well as of the amount of wealth creation through the job.

## 4 धर्मेण जयति लोकान् ।

*dharmeṇa jayati lokān*

(He) wins over the people through ethics.

The leader, the CEO and all other managers need to earn the trust and the loyalty of their followers, their colleagues, and their employees. Only when such a trust exists, will their work plans be understood in the right perspective and implemented in the proper manner to reach or to even exceed the desired gaol. The only way to win such trust, to win over his people and the society to his side, supporting his cause, is to ensure a totally ethical behaviour. The strong growth of corporate governance ideas after 1980, the current insistence of ethical codes of conduct for all employees etc. are manifestations of the same idea. In the jungle of market economy, civilisation would come only through ethical behaviour by all enterprises.

5 आत्मविनाशं सूचयति अधर्मबुद्धिः ।

*ātma-vināśaṁ sūcayati a-dharma-buddhiḥ*

Wanting to be unethical indicates self-destruction.

The temptation to act un-ethical, or at least non-ethically, is often strong, because such actions clearly give much larger gains than by following the virtuous path. These gains need not only be monetary or wealth related; these could be any type of gratification of desires. In the short-term, immediate fulfilment of the desire by any means irrespective of ethical considerations does give substantial pleasure. It is only the consequences of such non-ethical behaviour that are bad for the erring individual. These consequences manifest themselves in the long term, and are of many kinds. Those adversely affected would retaliate; the trust that was built over the years would be lost, the work assignments under his guidance would become difficult to handle and would often fail, his adversaries within the organisation would want to remove him from the position which he has misused etc. All such consequences invariably lead to the downfall of the managers who behave unethically. In his typical way, Cāṇakya only points out that temptation to behave unethically is the sure way for a manager to get oneself destroyed. The manager himself is thus inviting self-destruction.

6 न अस्ति अहंकारसमः शत्रुः ।

*na asti ahaṅkara-samaḥ śatruḥ*

There exists no enemy which equals egotism.

Temptations for doing something unethical can - and often do - arise in the minds of those in power position. However, good managers do not let such thoughts get converted into reality. They stem the thoughts at the same level, and use rational thinking with empathy to stay on the righteous path. Only the arrogant manager, cock sure of his capability and prowess, over confident about his abilities to manage his unethical action stealthily; and disdainful of the capability of others, will go ahead and commit some of the unethical deeds that he happens to have thought of. Such a strong ego, egotism at its worst, is truly the enemy of the manager.

As we have seen right in the beginning, humility is a necessary quality of the leader-manager. It permits him to listen carefully, to accept sound advice from others etc. The arrogant manager would not behave like this – he will fail to benefit from others. His egotism itself will work against him, leading to his failure. "Do not let this enemy, egotism, conquer you" is the advice.

## 7 दुर्दर्शनाः हि राजानः प्रजा नाशयन्ति ।

*durdarśanāḥ hi rājānaḥ prajā nāśyanti*

Immoral/non-virtuous (kings) chiefs indeed destroy the (subjects) employees.

Obviously, Cāṇakya is not talking about the 'looks' of a chief here, though ugly or ill-looking is the common meaning of the word *dur-darśanāḥ*. The relevant meanings of *darśana* here are: examination, inspection, discernment, intellect, judgement; virtue, moral merit; and possibly intention. If the CEO himself lacks many of these capabilities, the enterprise cannot really survive, certainly not in the long term. Then all stakeholders lose, the employees suffer the maximum loss.

Those chiefs who are egoistic and non-ethical, are most likely to use their intelligence in selfish ways detrimental to the organisation and its goals.

8 सुदर्शनाः राजानः प्रजा रक्षन्ति ।

*su-darśanāḥ rājānaḥ prajā rakṣanti*

Ethical/virtuous chiefs protect employees.

The opposite of the negative statement of the previous *sūtra* has to be stated, and not taken for granted. While ethically correct chiefs will not wilfully take action which could harm the employees or the organisation, it is not inevitabe that they will take specific steps to protect them – i.e. to take steps for their all round welfare. This *sūtra* stresses this positive, proactive aspect of the role of the CEO. He must take steps such as paying well appropriately for job content, providing good working conditions, implementing a good rewards and punishment policy etc. The basic idea is not to wait for complaints to arise or for demands to be raised for getting such fair needs satisfied.

9 न्याययुक्तं राजानम् मातरम् मन्यते प्रजा ।

*nyāya-yuktaṁ rajanaṁ mātaraṁ manyate prajā*

A just/righteous (king) chief is considered to be (equated with) the mother by the (subjects) employees.

The ethical and virtuous chief strives continuously for ensuring good wealth generation through getting all employees to work for the organisational goals by motivating them through fair and just treatment. When, in the long run, he is perceived by all to be a fair and just person providing good governance without exception, he is revered like a mother. The mother's image here is apt: she has only the welfare of her children at heart, is often a strict disciplinarian, but is always close to the children in their relationship. In the Indian/oriental cultural setting, the comparison of their chief with mother is indeed paying the highest regard and compliment.

## 10 तादृशः स राजा इह सुखं ततः स्वर्गम् च आप्नोति ।

*tādṛśaḥ sa rājā iha sukhaṁ tataḥ svargaṁ ca āpnoti*

The king like that begets happiness here, and heaven hereafter.

This *sūtra* can be considered to be the last of all the *sūtra* by Cāṇakya on management. As mentioned in the introduction, the *sūtras* reproduced here as the last 4-5 chapters are not found contagiously with those in the first 15-16 chapters. However, their order of appearance amongst the over 450 *sūtras* turned out to be nearly the same as used in the present text. This is a lucky coincidence, indicating that the thought flow of Cāṇakya was indeed on the same lines as here.

Let us note the ending: the chief, the leader, the manager will be happy in this world. No mention has been made of fame, wealth etc. After all, the most cherished and the most sought after goal of every human being is happiness. Happiness, as a continuous steady state of mind, is something which only a small minority of human being are seen to enjoy. At the apex level of any hierarchy (perhaps other than in religious orders), such a happy state of mind is difficult to achieve and therefore, extremely rarely found. Even when achieved, it is difficult to maintain. It is for this reason that Cāṇakyas scheme for training of top management incorporates the philosophical principles such as *sānkhya* and *yoga*, as well as the concepts of conquering of self and control over organs of sense and action. Only a person who has internalised these principles of life will be able to achieve happiness for himself through making all others also happy in their lives. And how is such happiness achieved?

॥ सुखस्य मूलम् धर्मः ॥

॥ *sukhasya mūlam dharmah* ॥

॥ Happiness is Rooted in Ethics ॥

***Sūtra* Summary: Ethics**

The world is looked after through ethics. Empathy is the mother of ethics. Truth and payment are based in ethics. (The chief) wins people over by ethics. Non-ethical inclination leads to self-destruction. No enemy like egotism. Immoral, non-discerning chiefs destroy employees. Virtuous chiefs protect their employees proactively. A just and fair chief is revered like mother. Such chiefs beget happiness in this world and reach heaven hereafter.

# *Sūtra* Listing

1.1 सुखस्य मूलं धर्मः ।
1.2 धर्मस्य मूलम् अर्थः ।
1.3 अर्थस्य मूलम् राज्यम् ।
1.4 राज्यमूलम् इंद्रियजयः ।
1.5 इन्द्रियजयस्य मूलम् विनयः ।
1.6 विनयस्य मूलम् वृद्धोपसेवा ।
1.7 वृद्धोपसेवया विज्ञानम् ।
1.8 विज्ञानेन आत्मानम् संपादयेत् ।
1.9 संपादितात्मा जितात्मा भवति ।
1.10 जितात्मा सर्वार्थैः संयुज्येत ।

2.1 अर्थसंपत् प्रकृतिसंपदं करोति ।
2.2 प्रकृतिसंपदा अनायकं अपि राज्यं नीयते ।
2.3 प्रकृतिकोपः सर्वकोपेभ्यो गरीयान् ।
2.4 अविनीतस्वामिलाभात् अस्वामिलाभः श्रेयान् ।
2.5 संपाद्य आत्मानम् अन्विच्छेत् सहायवान् ।
2.6 न असाहयस्य मंत्रनिश्चयः ।
2.7 न एकं चक्रं भ्रामयति ।
2.8 सहायः समसुखदुःखः ।
2.9 गानी प्रतिमानिनम् आत्मनि द्वितीयं मन्त्रम् उत्पादयेत् ।
2.10 अविनीतं स्नेहमात्रेण न मन्त्रे कुर्वीत ।
2.11 श्रुतवन्तम् उपधाशुद्धम् मंत्रिणम् कुर्वीत ।

3.1 मंत्रमूलाः सर्वारम्भाः।

3.2 मन्त्ररक्षणे कार्यसिद्धिः भवति ।

3.3 मंत्रविस्रावी कार्यं नाशयति ।

3.4 प्रमादात् द्विषतां वशम् उपयास्यति ।

3.5 सर्वद्वारेभ्यः मन्त्रो रक्षितव्य ।

3.6 मन्त्रसंपदा राज्यम् वर्धते ।

3.7 श्रेष्ठतमाम् मंत्रगुप्तिम् आहुः ।

3.8 कार्यान्धस्य प्रदीपः मन्त्रः ।

3.9 मन्त्रचक्षुषा परच्छिद्राणि अवलोकयन्ति ।

3.10 मन्त्रकाले मत्सरः न कर्तव्यः ।

3.11 त्रयाणम् एकवाक्ये संप्रत्ययः।

3.12 कार्याकार्यतत्वार्थदर्शिनः मन्त्रिणः ।

3.13 षट्कर्णात भिद्यते मन्त्रः ।

4.1 आपत्सु स्नेहसंयुक्तं मित्रं ।

4.2 मित्रसंग्रहणे बलं संपाद्यते ।

4.3 बलवान् अलब्धलाभे प्रयतते ।

4.4 अलब्धलाभः न अलसस्य ।

4.5 अलसस्य लब्धम् अपि रक्षितुं न शक्यते ।

4.6 न च अलसस्य रक्षितं विवर्धते ।

4.7 न भृत्यान् प्रेषयति ।

4.8 अलब्धलाभादि चतुष्टयं राज्यतंत्रम् ।

5.1 राज्यतंत्रायत्तम् नीतिशास्त्रम् ।

5.2 राज्यतन्त्रेषु आयत्तौ तंत्रावापौ ।

5.3 तन्त्रम् स्वविषयकृत्येषु आयत्तम् ।

5.4 आवापः मंडलनिविष्टः ।

5.5 सन्धिविग्रहयोः निर्मण्डलः ।
5.6 नीतिशास्त्रानुगः राजा ।
5.7 अनन्तरप्रकृतिः शत्रुः ।
5.8 एकान्तरितं मित्रम् इष्यते ।
5.9 हेतुतः शत्रुमित्रे भविष्यतः ।

6.1 हीयमानः सन्धिम् कुर्वीत ।
6.2 हीयमानेन न सन्धिम् कुर्वीत ।
6.3 तेजो हि सन्धानहेतुः तदर्थानाम् ।
6.4 न अतप्तलोहः लोहेन संधीयते ।
6.5 बलवान् हीनेन विगृण्हीयात् ।
6.6 न ज्यायसा समेन या ।
6.7 गजपादयुद्धम् इव बलवद्विग्रहः ।
6.8 आमपात्रम् आमेन सह विनश्यति ।
6.9 अरिप्रयत्नम् अभिसमीक्षेत ।
6.10 सन्धाय एकतः वा ।
6.11 अमित्रविरोधात् आत्मरक्षाम् आवसेत् ।
6.12 द्वयः अपि ईर्ष्यतः द्वैधीभावं कुर्वीत ।

7.1 शक्तिहीनः बलवन्तम् आश्रयेत् ।
7.2 दुर्बलाश्रयः दुःखम् आवहति ।
7.3 अग्निवत् राजानं आश्रयेत् ।
7.4 राज्ञः प्रतिकूलं न आचरेत् ।
7.5a उद्धतवेषधरः न भवेत् ।
7.6a न देवचरितं चरेत् ।
7.5 दुर्बलः अपि राजा न अवमन्तव्यः ।
7.6 न अस्ति अग्नौ दौर्बल्यम् ।

7.7 न व्यसनपरस्य कार्यावाप्तिः ।

7.8 इन्द्रियवशवर्ती चतुरंगवान् अपि विनश्यति। इन्द्रियवशवर्तिनि न अस्ति कार्याव्याप्तिः।

7.9 न अस्ति कार्यम् द्युतप्रवृत्तस्य ।

7.10 मृगयापरस्य धर्मार्थौ विनश्यतः ।

7.11 अर्थेषणा न व्यसनेषु गण्यते ।

7.12 न कामासक्तस्य कार्यानुष्ठानम् ।

8.1 अग्निदाहात् अपि विशिष्ठं वाकपारुष्यम् ।

8.2 दण्डपारुष्यात् सर्वजनद्वेष्यः भवति ।

8.3 अमित्रः दण्डनीत्याम् आयत्तः ।

8.4 दण्डनीतिम् अधितिष्ठन् प्रजा संरक्षिता ।

8.5 दण्डः संपदा योजयति ।

8.6 दण्डाभावे मन्त्रिवर्गाभावः ।

8.7 न दण्डात् अकार्याणि कुर्वन्ति ।

8.8 दण्डनीत्याम् आयत्तम् आत्मरक्षणं ।

8.9 आत्मनि रक्षिते सर्वं रक्षितं भवति ।

8.10 आत्मायतौ वृद्धिविनाशौ ।

8.11 दण्डः हि विज्ञाने प्रणीयते ।

8.12 दण्डे प्रणीयते वृत्तिः ।

9.1 वृत्तिमूलं अर्थलाभः ।

9.2 अर्थमूलौ धर्मकामौ ।

9.3 अर्थमूलं कार्यम् ।

9.4 यत् अल्पप्रयत्नात् कार्यसिद्धिः भवति ।

9.5 सर्वाः च संपद् सर्वोपायेन परिग्रहेत् ।

9.6 अर्थतोषिणं श्रीः परित्यजति ।

9.7 भाग्यवन्तम् अपरीक्ष्यकारिणम् श्रीः परित्यजति ।
9.8 ज्ञानानुमानैः च परीक्षा कर्तव्या ।

10.1 उपायपूर्वं न दुष्करं स्यात् ।
10.2 अनुपायपूर्वं कार्यं कृतमपि नश्यति ।
10.3 कार्यार्थिनाम् उपायः एव सहायः ।
10.4 कार्यं पुरुषकारेण लक्ष्यं संपद्यते ।
10.5 पुरुषकारम् अनुवर्तते दैवम् ।
10.6 दैवं विना अतिप्रयत्नं करोति यत् तद् विफलम् ।
10.7 पूर्वं निश्चित्य पश्चात् कार्यं आरभेत् ।
10.8 कार्यान्तरे दीर्घसूत्रता न कर्तव्या ।
10.9 असमाहितस्य वृत्तिः न विद्यते ।
10.10 न चलचित्तस्य कार्याव्याप्तिः ।
10.11 हस्तागतावमानात् कार्यव्यतिक्रमो भवति ।

11.1 दोषवर्जितानि कार्याणि दुर्लभानि ।
11.2 दुरनुबन्धम् कार्यम् न आरभेत् ।
11.3 कालविद् कार्यम् साधयेत् ।
11.4 कालातिक्रमात् कालः एव कार्यं पिबति ।
11.5 क्षणं प्रति कालविक्षेपम् न कुर्यात् सर्वकृत्येषु ।
11.6 देशकालविभागौ ज्ञात्वा कार्यम् आरभेत् ।
11.7 दैवहीनम् कार्यम् सुसाधम् अपि दुःसाधं भवति ।
11.8 नीतिज्ञः देशकालौ परीक्षेत ।
11.9 परीक्ष्यकारिणी श्रीः चिरं तिष्ठति ।

12.1 दुःसाधम् अपि सुसाधं करोति उपायज्ञः ।
12.2 यः यस्मिन् कार्ये कुशलः तं तस्मिन् एव योजयेत् ।
12.3 अज्ञानिना कृतम् अपि न बहु मन्तव्यम् ।

12.4 यादृच्छिकत्वात् कृमिः अपि रूपान्तराणि करोति ।
12.5 सिद्धस्य इव कार्यस्य प्रकाशनम् कर्तव्यम् ।
12.6 ज्ञानवताम् अपि दैवमानुषदोषात् कार्याणि दुष्यन्ति ।
12.7 दैवदोषम् शान्तिकर्मणा प्रतिषेधयेत् ।
12.8 मानुषीं कार्यविपत्तीम् कौशलेन विनिवारयेत् ।
12.9 कार्यविपत्तौ दोषान् वर्णयन्ति बालिशाः ।
12.10 कार्यार्थिना दाक्षिण्यं न कर्तव्यम् ।
12.11 क्षीरार्थी वत्सः मातुः उधः प्रतिहन्ति ।
12.12 अप्रयत्नात् कार्यविपत्तिः भवति ।
12.13 न दैवप्रमाणानां कार्यसिद्धिः ।
12.14 कार्यबहुत्वे बहुफलम् आयतिकम् कुर्यात् ।
12.15 स्वयम् एव अवस्कन्नं कार्यम् निरीक्षेत् ।

13.1 कार्यबाह्यः न पोषयति आश्रितान् ।
13.2 यः कार्यम् न पश्यति सः अन्धः ।
13.3 प्रत्यक्षपरोक्षानुमानैः कार्याणि परीक्षेत ।
13.4 अपरीक्ष्यकारिणं श्रीः परित्यजति ।
13.5 परीक्ष्य तार्या विपत्तिः ।
13.6 स्वशक्तिम् ज्ञात्वा कार्यम् आरभेत् ।
13.7 स्वजनं तर्पयित्वा यः शेषभोजी सः अमृतभोजी ।
13.8 सम्यग् अनुष्ठानात् आयमुखानि वर्धन्ते ।

14.1 न अस्ति भीरोः कार्यचिन्ता ।
14.2 स्वामिनः शीलं ज्ञात्वा कार्यार्थी कार्यम् साधयेत् ।
14.3 धेनोः शीलज्ञः हि क्षीरं भूङक्ते ।
14.4 क्षुद्रे गुह्यप्रकाशनम् आत्मवान् न कुर्यात् ।
14.5 आश्रितैः अपि अवमन्यते मृदुस्वभावः ।

14.6 तीक्ष्णदण्डः सर्वैः उद्वेजनीयः भवति ।

14.7 यथार्हदण्डकारी स्यात् ।

14.8 अल्पसारम् श्रुतवन्तम् अपि न बहुमन्यते लोकः ।

14.9 अतिभारः पुरुषम् अवसादयति ।

15.1 यःसंसदि परदोषान् शंसति सः स्वदोषं प्रख्यापयति ।

15.2 आत्मानम् एव नाशयति आत्मवताम् कोपः ।

15.3 न अस्ति अप्राप्यं सत्यव्रताम् !

15.4 न केवलेन साहसेन कार्यसिद्धिः भवति ।

15.5 साहसे खलु श्रीः वसति ।

15.6 व्यसनार्तः विस्मरति अवश्यकर्तव्यान् ।

15.7 न अस्ति अन्तरायः कालविक्षेपे ।।

15.8 असंशयविनाशात् संशयविनाशः श्रेयान् ।

16.1 केवलं धनानि निक्षेप्तुः न स्वार्थः न दानं न धर्मः ।

16.2 दानं धर्मः ।

16.3 अपरधनानपेक्षं केवलं अर्थदानं श्रेयः ।

16.4 न आर्यगतः अर्थवृद्धिपरीतः अनर्थभावः ।

16.5 न्यायागतः अर्थः ।

16.6 तद् विपरीतः अर्थाभासः ।

16.7 यः धर्मार्थौ न पीडयति सः कामः

16.8 तद् विपरीतः कामाभासः ।

16.9 तद् विपरीतः अनर्थसेवी ।

16.10 अवमानेन आगतं ऐश्वर्यं अवमन्यते साधुः ।

17.1 ऋजुस्वभावपरः जनेषु दुर्लभः ।

17.2 गुणवदाश्रयात् निर्गुणः अपि गुणी भवति ।

17.3 क्षीराश्रितम् जलम् क्षीरम् एव भवति ।
17.4 महात्मना परेण साहसं न कर्तव्यम् ।
17.5 कदाचित् अपि चरित्रं न लंघयेत् ।
17.6 क्षुधार्तः न तृणं चरति सिंहः ।
17.7 प्राणात् अपि प्रत्ययः रक्षितव्यः ।
17.8 पिशुनः नेता पुत्रदारैः अपि त्यज्यते ।
17.9 बालात् अपि अर्थजातम् श्रुणुयात् ।
17.10 सत्यम् अपि अश्रद्धेयम् न वदेत् ।

18.1 बहून् अपि गुणान् एकदोषः ग्रसति ।
18.2 न अल्पदोषात् बहुगुणाः त्यज्यन्ते ।
18.3 विपश्चित्सु अपि सुलभाः दोषाः ।
18.4 न अस्ति रत्नम् अखण्डितम् ।
18.5 मर्यादातीतम् न कदाचित् अपि विश्वसेत् ।
18.6 अप्रिये कृते प्रियम् अपि द्वेष्यम् भवति ।
18.7 नमन्ति अपि तुलाकोटिः कूपोदकक्षयं करोति ।
18.8 सताम् मतम् न अतिक्रमेत् ।

19.1 उत्साहवताम् शत्रवः अपि वशीभवन्ति ।
19.2 विक्रमधनाः हि राजानः ।
19.3 न अस्ति अलसस्य ऐहिकं आमुष्मिकं वा ।
19.4 निरुत्साहात् दैवम् पतति ।
19.5 आत्मच्छिद्रम् न प्रकाशयेत् ।
19.6 छिद्रप्रहरणः शत्रवः अपि ।
19.7 स्वजनस्य दुर्वृत्तम् निवारयेत् ।
19.8 एकाङ्गदोषः पुरुषम् अवसादयति !
19.9 कम् अपि पुरुषम् न अवमन्येत ।

19.10 क्षन्तव्यं इति पुरुषम् न बाधेत ।

19.11 कार्यसंकटेषु अर्थव्यवसायिनी बुद्धिः ।

20.1 स्वजनेषु अतिक्रमः न कर्तव्यः ।

20.2 माता अपि दुष्टा त्याज्या ।

20.3 स्वहस्तः अपि विषदिग्घः छेद्यः ।

20.4 अप्रतीकारेषु अनादरः न कर्तव्यः

20.5 परः अपि च हितः बन्धुः ।

20.6 गुणे न मत्सरः कर्तव्यः ।

20.7 संसदि शत्रुं न परिक्रोशेत् ।

20.8 शत्रोः अपि सुगुणाः ग्राह्याः ।

20.9 चिरपरिचितानाम् अत्युपचारः शंकितव्यः ।

20.10 अतिसंगः दोषम् उत्पादयाति ।

21.1 धर्मेण धार्यते लोकः ।

21.2 दया धर्मस्य जन्मभूमिः ।

21.3 धर्ममूले सत्यदाने ।

21.4 धर्मेण जयति लोकान् ।

21.5 आत्मविनाशं सूचयति अधर्मबुद्धिः ।

21.6 न अस्ति अहंकारसमः शत्रुः ।

21.7 दुर्दर्शनाः हि राजानः प्रजा नाशयन्ति ।

21.8 सुदर्शनाः राजानः प्रजा रक्षन्ति ।

21.9 न्याययुक्तं राजानम् मातरम् मन्यते प्रजा ।

21.10 तादृशः स राजा इह सुखं ततः स्वर्गम् च आप्नोति ।

# References


1. Encarta Encyclopedia by Microsoft PP-1
2. Kautiliya Arthashastra by R. P. Kangle, Motilal Barasidas, Delhi. PP-8
3. Human Society in Ethics by Bertrand Russell, Routledge, London. PP-15
4. Vidura Neeti, Udyoga Parva, Mahabharata. PP-16
5. Thirukkural by Kasturi Sreenivasan, Bharatiya Vidya Bhavan, Mumbai. PP-16
6. Bhartruhari Shataka, Ed. Pandit Rakesh Sadhana Pocket Books, Delhi. PP-21
7. Srimad Bhagavadgeeta, with English translation, Gita Press, Gorakhpur. PP-23
8. In Search of Excellence, by TJ Peters and RH Waterman, Harper & Row, Publisher. New York PP-29
9. Patanjala Yogadarshan, with Marathi critique, KK Kolhatkar, KB Dhavale Publishers, Mumbai. PP-82
10. Panchatantra, Sanskrit, critique by Narayan Ram Acharya, Nirnaysagar Press, Mumbai. PP-202
11. Mahabharata, Bhandarkar Oriental Research Institute, Pune. PP-239